United States
Department of
Agriculture

Forest Service

**Northern
Research Station**

Resource Bulletin
NRS-72

Minnesota Timber Industry: An Assessment of Timber Product Output and Use

2007

David E. Haugen
Keith Jacobson

Abstract

In 2007, there were 417 primary wood-processing mills in Minnesota, five more mills than in 2004. These mills processed 229.8 million cubic feet of industrial roundwood, of which 207.8 million cubic feet were harvested from within the State. Another 9.1 million cubic feet of the industrial roundwood harvested in Minnesota were sent to primary wood-processing mills in other states and Canada. Pulpwood accounted for 77 percent of the total harvest. The harvesting of industrial roundwood products produced 108.1 million cubic feet of logging residues. Primary wood-processing mills generated 1.5 million green tons of mill residues, with 63 percent of the mill residues being used for industrial fuel. Only 1.1 percent of the mill residues were not used for other products.

Cover Photo

Photo by U.S. Forest Service.

Contents

INTRODUCTION

Minnesota's wood products manufacturing industry employs more than 28,442 workers with an output of about $8.7 billion (NAICS 321—Wood product manufacturing, and NAICS 322—Paper manufacturing) (U.S. Census Bureau 2007). Given the economic importance of the State's wood product industry, this bulletin analyzes recent Minnesota forest industry trends and reports the results of a detailed study of the forest product industry, industrial roundwood production, and associated primary mill wood and bark residue production in Minnesota in 2007. Such detailed information is necessary for long-range planning and decisionmaking in wood procurement, economic research, forest resources management, and forest industry development. Likewise, researchers utilize current forest industry and industrial roundwood information for assessing future research needs and project development.

The 2004 Timber Industrial Assessment for Minnesota (Reading and Jacobson 2008) was used as a primary baseline of comparison for results. As a result of our ongoing efforts to improve the timber product output (TPO) survey's efficiency and reliability, minor changes in previously published data (e.g., Reading and Jacobsen 2008) may have occurred due to omissions and/or correction of errors with the reprocessing of earlier data. Rows and columns of supporting tables in the current report may not sum due to rounding, but data in each table cell are accurately displayed.

Information about the forest land resource of Minnesota is available at the Forest Inventory and Analysis Web site at: http://nrs.fs.fed.us/fia/data-tools/state-reports/MN.

The Authors

DAVID E. HAUGEN is a forester with the U.S. Forest Service, Forest Inventory and Analysis Program, Northern Research Station, St. Paul, MN.

KEITH JACOBSON is the forest product utilization and marketing program leader, Minnesota Department of Natural Resources, St. Paul, MN.

STUDY METHODS

This study was a cooperative effort between the Minnesota Department of Natural Resources (MN-DNR) and the Forest Inventory and Analysis (FIA) program at the Northern Research Station (NRS) of the U.S. Forest Service. The FIA program is responsible for providing forest resource statistics for all ownerships across the United States, including timber product outputs.

MN-DNR surveyed all know primary wood-using mills using questionnaires designed to determine the size and composition of the State's primary wood-using industry, its use of roundwood, and its generation and disposition of wood residues. The responses from the questionnaires were entered into a database and sent to NRS for additional processing and analyzing. As part of data processing, all industrial roundwood volumes reported on the questionnaires were converted to standard units of measure using regional conversion factors (Table 1). Timber removals by source of material and harvest residues generated during logging were estimated from standard product volumes using factors developed from previous NRS logging utilization studies. Minnesota's industrial roundwood receipts data along with out-of state uses of Minnesota roundwood were integrated with a regional timber removals database to provide a complete assessment of Minnesota's timber product output.

Certain terms used in this report—retained, export, import, production, and receipts— have specialized meanings and relationships unique to the FIA program that surveys timber product output (TPO) (Fig. 1).

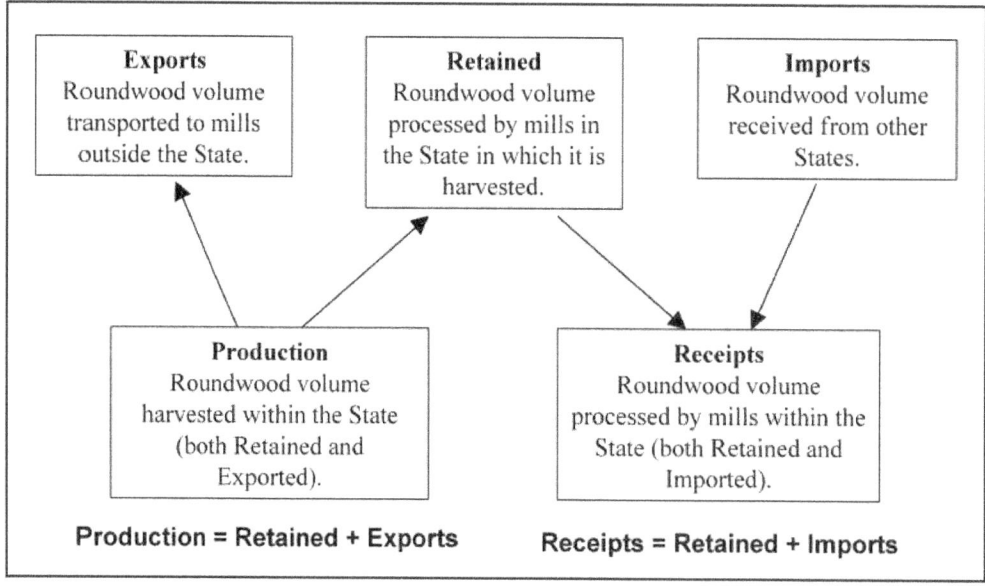

Figure 1.—Diagram of the movement of industrial roundwood.

Table 1.—Conversion factors from reported unit of measure to standard unit of measure[a]

Reported unit of measure

Product (Standard unit of measure)	International ¼-inch rule MBF	Doyle scale MBF	Green tons	Standard cords	Thousand pieces	Thousand cubic feet
Saw logs and handles (MBF International ¼-inch rule)	1	1.38	0.2174	0.5		0.158
Veneer logs and cooperage (MBF International ¼-inch rule)	1	1.14		0.5		0.158
Pulp and composite products, and industrial fuelwood (Standard cords)			0.4167	1		0.079
Mine timbers (Thousand cubic feet)		0.2322		0.079	6.7	1
Poles (Pieces)	20		4.348	10	1,000	0.0079
Posts (Thousand pieces)	0.2		0.04167	0.1	1	0.79
Cabin logs, excelsior/shavings, and miscellaneous products (Thousand cubic feet)	0.158	0.21804	0.0329193	0.079	7.9	1

[a] Reported volume times conversion factor = Standard volume.

PRIMARY TIMBER INDUSTRY IN MINNESOTA
Industrial Roundwood

- In 2007, Minnesota's primary wood-using industry included 368 sawmills, 2 veneer mills, 13 pulp and composite product mills, and 34 mills that produced other products (e.g., cabin logs, cooperage, excelsior, shavings, post and poles) (Table 2 and Fig. 2).

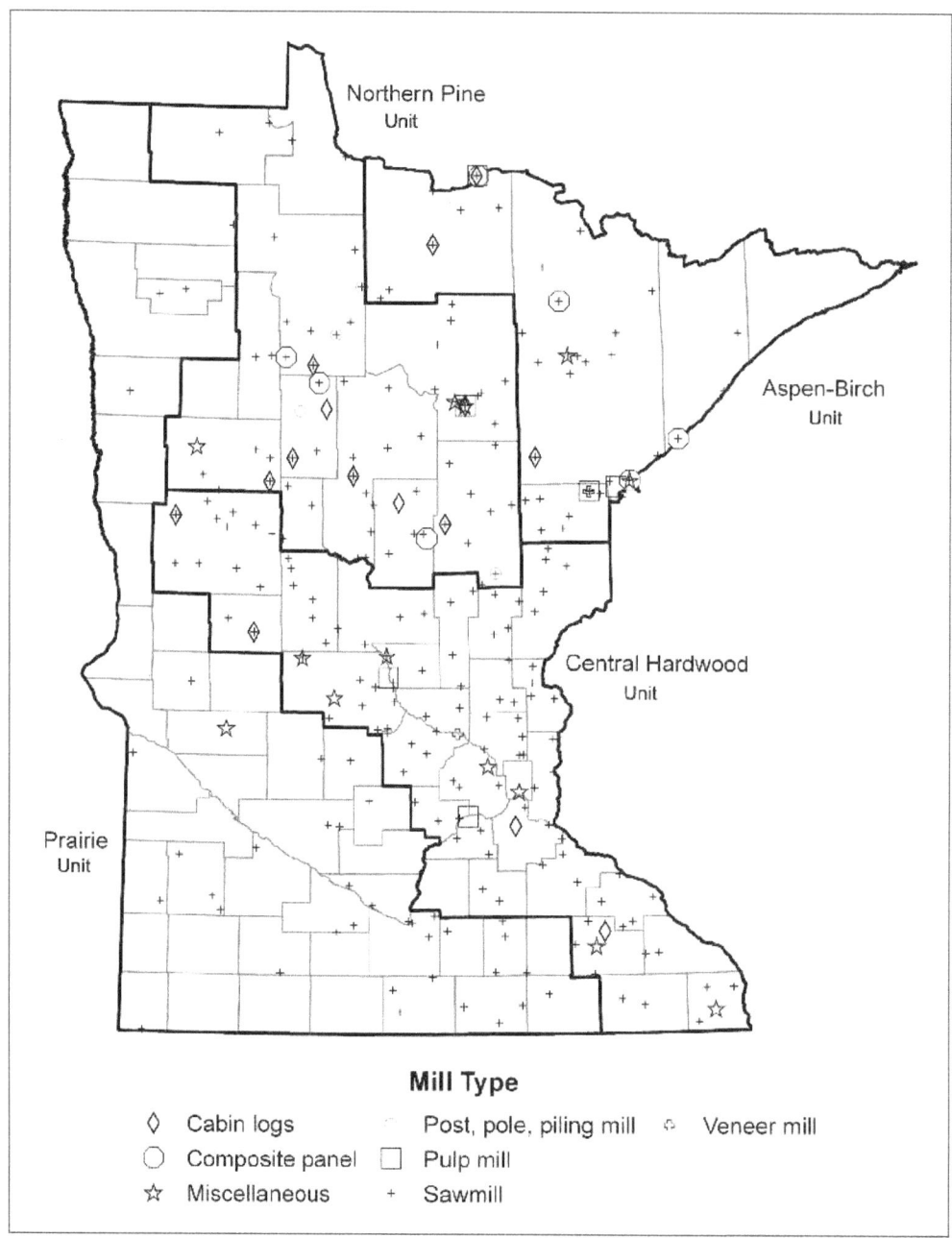

Mill Type

◇ Cabin logs	Post, pole, piling mill	⊙ Veneer mill
○ Composite panel	☐ Pulp mill	
☆ Miscellaneous	+ Sawmill	

Figure 2.—Primary wood-using mills by FIA Unit (heavy lines), Minnesota, 2007.

- Although total mills increased slightly (1 percent), the industry experienced losses in the large- and medium-size sawmills (two and seven sawmills, respectively) and one pulp mill. The number of small-size mills increased by 10 and the specialty mills (e.g., cabin log, cooperage, excelsior, shavings, post and poles) increased by five mills.

- Pulp mills process most of the roundwood in Minnesota. In 2007, the primary wood-using mills in Minnesota processed 229.8 million cubic feet of industrial roundwood with pulpwood accounting for more than 77 percent of the volume (Table 3).

- Ninety percent of the industrial roundwood processed by the State's primary wood-using mills was cut from Minnesota forest lands. Wisconsin was the largest supplier of out-of-State wood for Minnesota's forest products industry, providing 6 percent of the total industrial roundwood processed (Table 4).

- Seventy percent of the industrial roundwood processed by Minnesota primary wood-using mills were hardwood species. Aspen/balsam poplar alone accounted for 53 percent of the total volume processed. Other species of importance to the forest industry were red pine, spruce, balsam fir, jack pine, and white birch.

- Industrial roundwood production decreased by 20 percent, from 275.4 million cubic feet in 2004 to 219.1 million cubic feet in 2007 (Table 5 and Fig. 3).

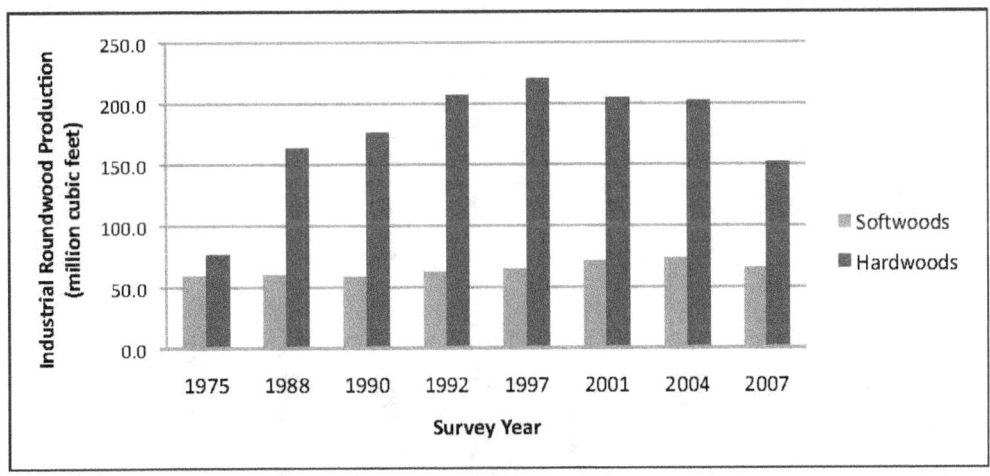

Figure 3.—Industrial roundwood production by softwoods and hardwoods, and survey year, Minnesota (Reading and Jacobson 2008, Reading and Krantz 2002, Hackett and Dahlman 1997, Hackett and Dahlman 1993, Smith and Dahlman 1991, Blyth et al. 1980).

- More than 90 percent of the 219.1 million cubic feet of industrial roundwood harvested in Minnesota was processed in the State (Table 6). Primary wood processors in Wisconsin received 4 percent of the industrial roundwood exported to other states. Other states receiving industrial roundwood harvested in Minnesota included Iowa, Ohio, Michigan, Indiana, South Dakota, and Missouri. Canadian industries also received roundwood harvested from Minnesota forest lands.

- In 2007, 51 percent, or 111.2 million cubic feet, of industrial roundwood was harvested from the Northern Pine Forest Inventory Unit (Table 7). Industrial roundwood harvests from the Aspen-Birch Unit were 37 percent (81.7 million cubic feet), the Central Hardwood Unit, 10 percent (22.7 million cubic feet) and the Prairie Unit, 2 percent (3.4 million cubic feet).

- The aspen/balsam poplar species group accounted for 53 percent of the total industrial roundwood harvested in 2007 (Fig. 4). Other important species harvested were spruce, white birch, red pine, balsam fir, and jack pine.

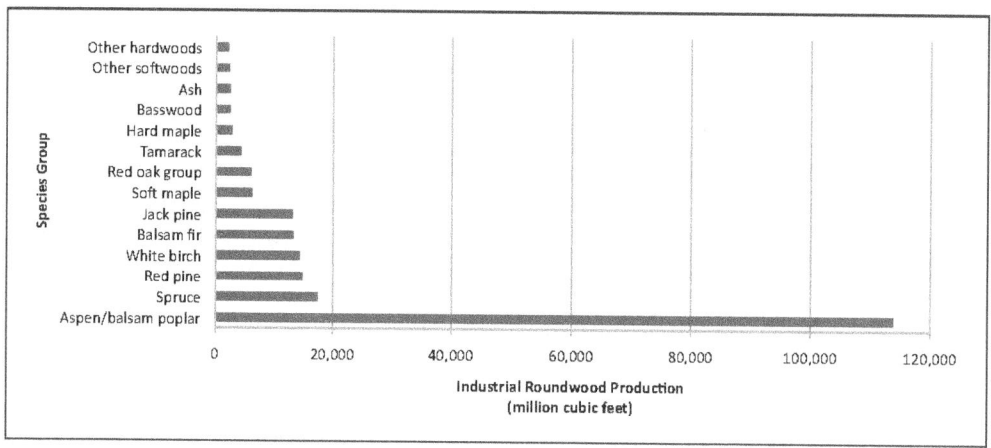

Figure 4.—Industrial roundwood production by species group, Minnesota, 2007.

- Pulpwood accounting for 77 percent of the total industrial roundwood harvested from Minnesota forests in 2007. Saw log harvests accounted for another 19 percent of the total industrial roundwood production in 2007 (Table 8 and Fig. 5).

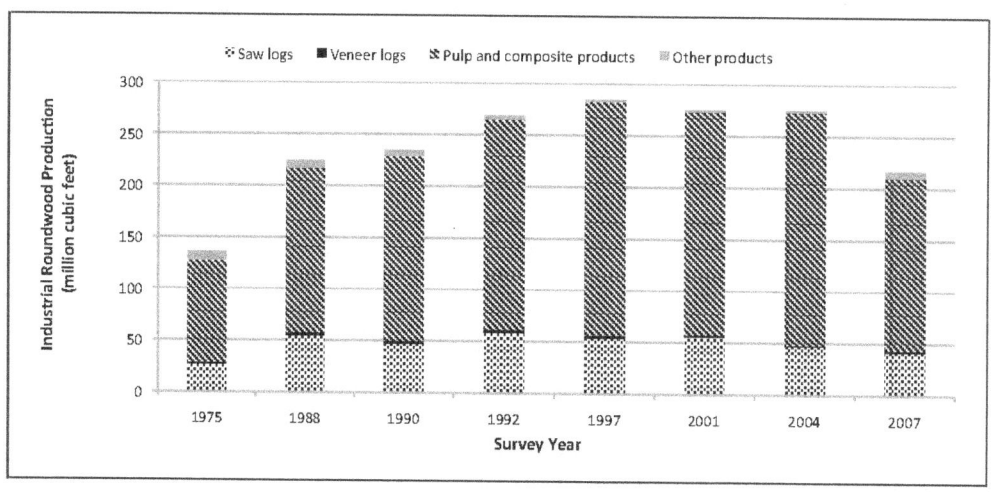

Figure 5.—Industrial roundwood production by product and survey year, Minnesota (Reading and Jacobson 2008, Reading and Krantz 2002, Hackett and Dahlman 1997, Hackett and Dahlman 1993, Smith and Dahlman 1991, Blyth et al. 1980).

Saw Logs

- Minnesota sawmill receipts totaled 239.5 million board feet in 2007, a decrease of 11 percent from 2004 (Table 9). Softwood saw log receipts decreased 8 percent to 150.1 million board feet, while those of hardwoods decreased 15 percent to 89.4 million board feet.

- Between the 2004 and 2007, red pine saw log receipts increased 18 percent, while jack pine and aspen saw log receipts declined by 35 and 34 percent, respectively.

- Saw log production decreased by 10 percent, from 257.1 million board feet in 2004 to 232.3 million board feet in 2007. Softwood saw log production decreased 8 percent to 134.9 million board feet, while those of hardwoods decreased 12 percent to 97.3 million board feet.

- In 2007, red pine accounted for almost 29 percent of the total harvest of saw logs from Minnesota forests. Other important species groups harvested were jack pine, red oaks, aspen/balsam poplar, spruce, and white birch (Fig. 6).

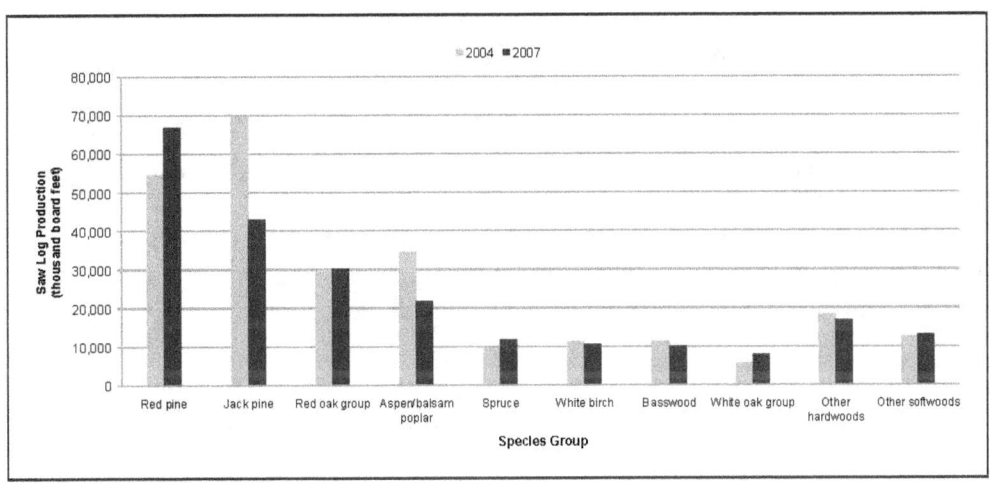

Figure 6.—Saw log production by species group, Minnesota, 2004 and 2007.

Other Products

- Pulpwood, at 166.7 million cubic feet, was the most harvested product from Minnesota forests in 2007. Pulpwood production increased by 25 percent between 2004 and 2007 (Table 5). The results of a separate Northern Region pulpwood study conducted for 2007 will appear in Piva (in prep.).

- Industrial fuelwood was the third most harvested industrial roundwood product in Minnesota in 2007. Production of industrial fuelwood was 3.6 million cubic feet in 2007.

- Other industrial roundwood products harvested from Minnesota in 2007 were veneer logs, excelsior shavings, cabin logs, poles, posts, cooperage, and other miscellaneous products. Combined, these products made up only 2 percent of the total volume of industrial roundwood produced.

- Residential fuelwood is not included in this report.

Timber Removals

- During the harvest of industrial roundwood from Minnesota's forests in 2007, 219.1 million cubic feet of wood material (growing stock such as sawtimber and pole timber, and non-growing stock such as limb wood, saplings, cull trees, dead trees) was used for primary wood products and another 109.2 million cubic feet of wood material (growing stock such as logging residue and non-growing stock such as logging slash) was left on the ground as harvest residues (Table 10 and Fig. 7).

- Growing-stock sources, at 218.3 million cubic feet, were the largest component of removals for industrial roundwood production. Ninety-four percent of the growing stock removed was used for products and 6 percent was left as harvest residue. Sawtimber-size trees accounted for 71 percent of the growing-stock volume that was used for products, and the remainder came from pole-size trees.

- In 2007, 110 million cubic feet of non-growing-stock wood material was removed in the production of industrial roundwood, but only 12 percent of this material was used for products and the remainder was left on the ground as logging slash. Fifty-nine percent of the non-growing-stock material used for industrial roundwood came from cull trees, and another 37 percent came from the limbs of growing-stock trees. The rest of the non-growing-stock material used for products came from dead trees and saplings (Table 10 and Fig. 7).

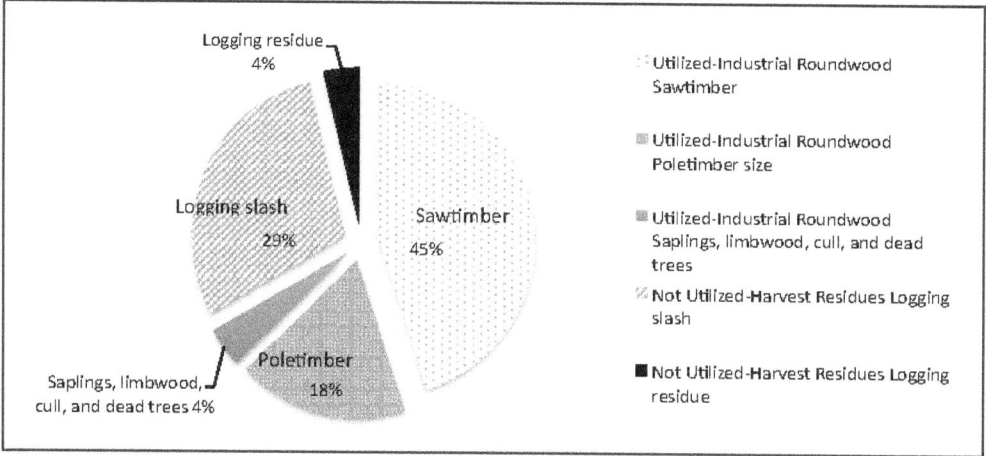

Figure 7.—Distribution of timber removals for industrial roundwood by source of material, Minnesota, 2007.

- Fifty-one percent of the total growing-stock material removed from Minnesota's timberland in 2007 came from the Northern Pine Forest Inventory Unit (Table 11), followed by the Aspen-Birch Unit with 37 percent, the Central Hardwoods Unit with 10 percent and the Prairie Unit with 2 percent of the total growing-stock volume removed.

- In 2007, 649.2 million board feet was removed from Minnesota's sawtimber inventory (Table 12). Aspen-balsam poplar accounted for 49 percent of the total sawtimber volume removed.

- The harvesting of industrial roundwood products from Minnesota forests in 2007 left 109.2 million cubic feet of harvest residues on the ground (Table 13).

Harvest Intensity

- Statewide in 2007, there was an average of 28.5 cubic feet of average annual net growth (gross growth minus mortality) of growing stock on timberland, and an average of 15.8 cubic feet of harvest-related wood removals per acre of forest land in Minnesota. Only 18 counties had more that 20 cubic feet of total wood material removed per acre of forest land (Fig. 8). (For reference, a cord of roundwood contains about 80 cubic feet of wood.)

- In 2007, there were 16.7 million acres of forest land in Minnesota (Miles and Heinzen 2008). The 2007 net volume in live trees on forest land was 17.9 billion cubic feet. The 328.4 million cubic feet of total wood material removed due to harvesting (Table 10) was 1.8 percent of the total live volume of trees on forest land in Minnesota.

- The Northern Pine Forest Inventory Unit had the greatest harvest intensity in 2007, with an average of 22 cubic feet of total wood removals per acre of forest land. Based on FIA data, private ownership accounted for 43 percent of the area of forest land and 41 percent of the average annual harvest removals (Miles 2011).

- The Aspen-Birch Unit had 17 cubic feet of total wood removals per acre of forest land. Harvesting had the greatest impact on privately owned forest land in this unit. FIA reports that 28 percent of the forest land in this unit was privately owned, but accounted for 40 percent of the average annual harvest removals.

- The Central Hardwoods Unit had 12 cubic feet of total wood removals per acre of forest land. FIA reports that 80 percent of the forest land in this unit was privately owned, accounting for 73 percent of the average annual harvest removals.

- The Prairie Unit had 9 cubic feet of total wood removals per acre of forest land. FIA reports that 79 percent of the forest land in this unit was privately owned, accounting for 82 percent of the average annual harvest removals.

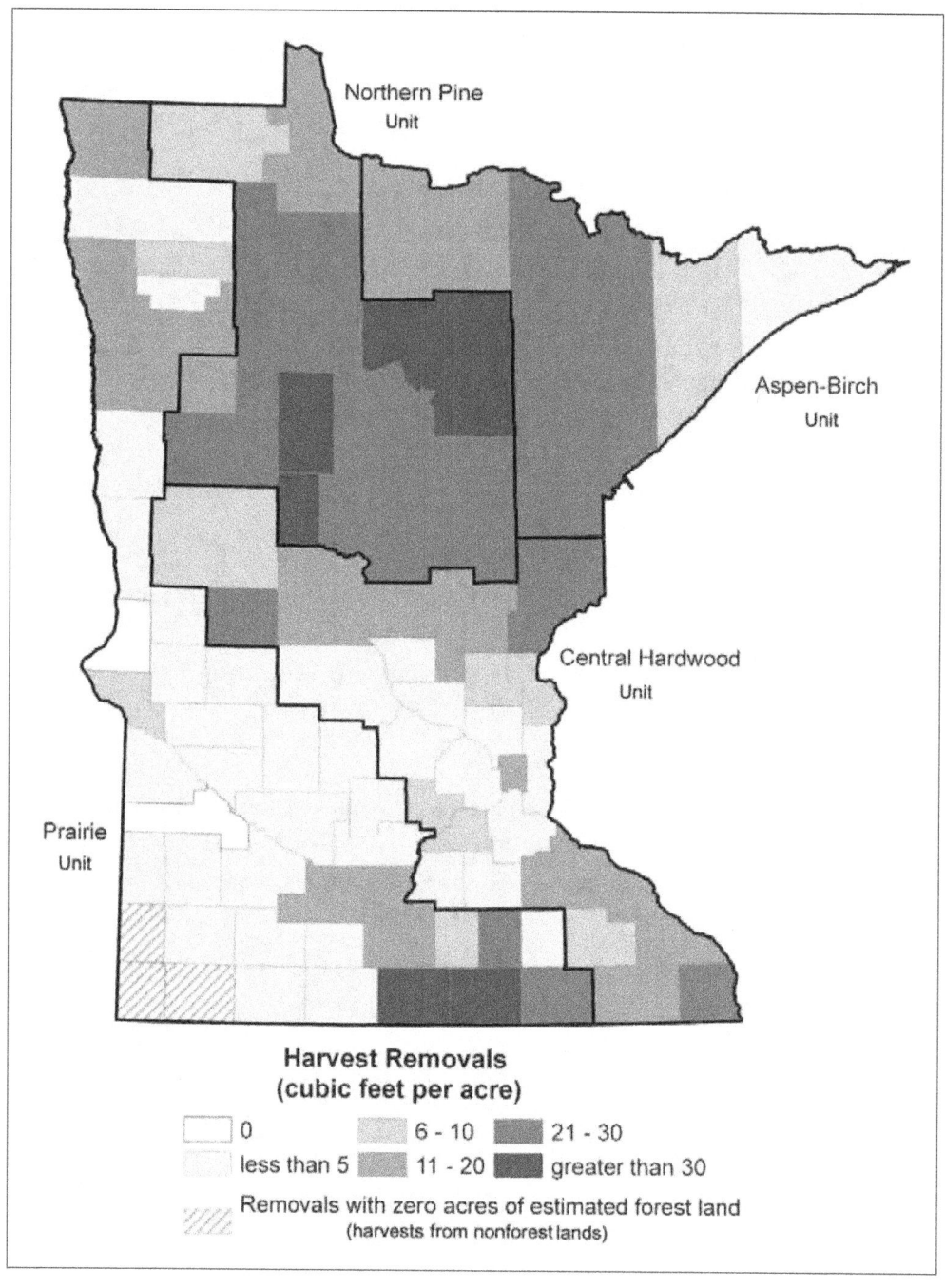

Figure 8.—Harvest removals of industrial roundwood, Minnesota, 2007.

Primary Mill Residues

- In converting industrial roundwood into products, such as lumber, wood pulp, and veneer, Minnesota's primary wood-using industries generated 1.48 million green tons of wood residue (coarse and fine residues) and bark residue (Table 14).

- Forty-nine percent of the mill residues were in the form of bark residue. Fine wood residue, such as sawdust or shavings, made up another 28 percent, and coarse wood residue, such as slabs and edgings, accounted for the remaining 23 percent (Fig. 9).

- Sixty-three percent of the mill residues were used for industrial fuel. Pulp and composite product mills consumed 11 percent of the mill residues; livestock bedding and domestic firewood consumed 8 percent each; miscellaneous use, including small dimension and specialty items, consumed 6 percent; and mulch consumed 3 percent of the mill residues generated. Only 1 percent of the mill residues generated by the primary wood processors of Minnesota went unused (Fig. 10).

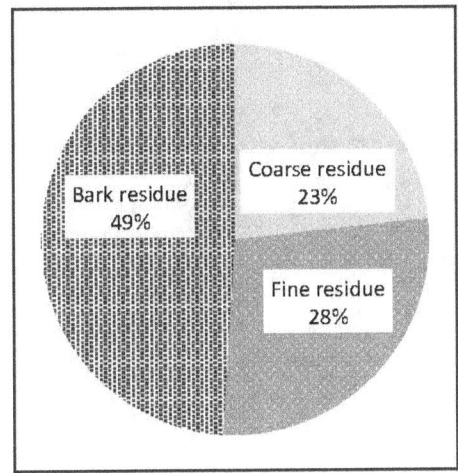

Figure 9.—Distribution of residues generated by primary wood-using mills by type of residue, Minnesota, 2007.

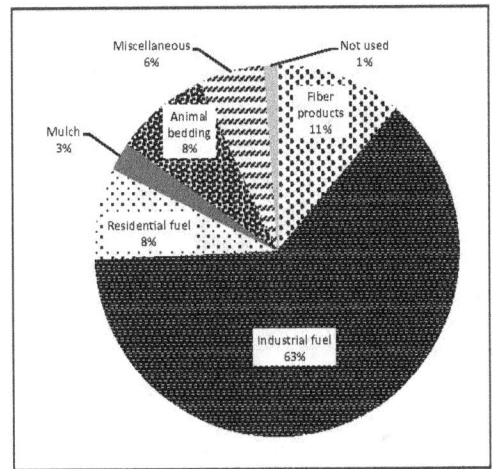

Figure 10.—Distribution of residues generated by primary wood-using mills by method of disposal, Minnesota, 2007.

- Eighty-four percent of the coarse residue was used by pulp and composite panel mills. Industrial fuelwood consumed 37 percent of the total fine residue generated, and 43 percent of the bark residue generated was used for mulch (Table 14).

ACKNOWLEDGMENTS

Special thanks are given to the primary wood-using firms for supplying information for this study and to the Minnesota Department of Natural Resources, Division of Forestry, whose cooperation in canvassing survey respondents is greatly appreciated.

Data processing was done by Ronald J. Piva, a forester with FIA, Northern Research Station, St. Paul, MN.

Figures 2 and 8 were created by Dale Gormanson, a forester with FIA, Northern Research Station, St. Paul, MN.

LITERATURE CITED

Blyth, J.E.; Whipple J.W.; Boelter A.H.; Wilhelm S. 1980. **Lake States primary forest industry and timber use, 1975.** Resour. Bull. NC-49. St. Paul, MN: U.S. Department of Agriculture, Forest Service, North Central Forest Experiment Station. 39 p.

Hackett, R.L.; Dahlman, R.A. 1993. **Minnesota timber industry--an assessment of timber product output and use, 1990.** Resour. Bull. NC-143. St. Paul, MN: U.S. Department of Agriculture, Forest Service, North Central Forest Experiment Station. 52 p.

Hackett, R.L.; Dahlman, R.A. 1997. **Minnesota timber industry—an assessment of timber product output and use, 1992.** Resour. Bull. NC-186. St. Paul, MN: U.S. Department of Agriculture, Forest Service, North Central Forest Experiment Station. 60 p.

Miles, P.D. 2011. **Forest Inventory EVALIDator web-application version 4.01 beta.** Newtown Square, PA: U.S. Department of Agriculture, Forest Service, Northern Research Station. Available at: http://fiatools.fs.fed.us/Evalidator4/tmattribute.jsp

Miles, P.D.; Heinzen, D. 2008. **Minnesota's forest resources, 2007.** Res. Note NRS-24. Newtown Square, PA: U.S. Department of Agriculture, Forest Service, Northern Research Station. 4 p.

Piva, Ronald J. [In prep]. **Pulpwood production in the northern region, 2007.** Resour. Bull. Newtown Square, PA: U.S. Department of Agriculture, Forest Service, Northern Research Station.

Reading, W. H., IV; Jacobson, K. 2008. **Minnesota timber industry—an assessment of timber product output and use, 2004.** Resour. Bull. NRS-25. Newtown Square, PA: U.S. Department of Agriculture, Forest Service, Northern Research Station. 74 p.

Reading, W.H., IV; Krantz, J., 2002. **Minnesota timber industry—an assessment of timber product output and use, 1997.** Resour. Bull. NC-204. St. Paul, MN: U.S. Department of Agriculture, Forest Service, North Central Research Station. 71 p.

Smith, W.B.; Dahlman, R., 1991. **Minnesota timber industry--an assessment of timber product output and use, 1988.** Resour. Bull. NC-127. St. Paul, MN: U.S. Department of Agriculture, Forest Service, North Central Forest Experiment Station. 61 p.

U. S. Census Bureau. 2007. **2007 Economic Census – Manufacturing – Minnesota.** http://factfinder.census.gov/servlet/IBQTable?_bm=y&-fds_name=EC0700A1&-geo_id=04000US27&-_skip=100&-ds_name=EC0731A1&-_lang=en (Accessed June 2011).

APPENDIX
Definition of Terms

Board foot. Unit of measure applied to roundwood. It corresponds to lumber that is 1 foot long, 1 foot wide, and 1 inch thick (or its equivalent).

Bolt. A short log no more than 8 feet long, to be sawn for lumber, peeled or sliced for veneer, shaved for excelsior, or converted into shingles, cooperage stock, dimension stock, blocks, blanks, or other products.

Central stem. The portion of a tree between a 1-foot stump and the minimum 4.0-inch top diameter outside bark, or point where the central stem breaks into limbs.

Coarse mill residue. Wood residue suitable for chipping such as slabs, edgings, and veneer cores.

Commercial species. Tree species presently or prospectively suitable for industrial wood products. (Note: Excludes species of typically small size, poor form, or inferior quality such as hophornbeam, Osage-orange, and redbud.)

Cull removals. Net volume of rough and rotten trees plus the net volume in sections of the central stem of growing-stock trees that do not meet regional merchantability standards but are harvested for industrial roundwood products.

Diameter at breast height (d.b.h.). The outside bark diameter at 4.5 feet above the forest floor on the uphill side of the tree. For determining breast height, the forest floor includes the duff layer that may be present, but does not include unincorporated woody debris that may rise above the ground line.

Doyle rule. A simple log rule or formula for estimating the board-foot volume of logs based on a 4-inch slabbing allowance to square the log. This rule is used in the eastern and southern United States.

Exports. The volume of roundwood utilized by mills outside the state where the timber was harvested.

Fine mill residue. Wood residue not suitable for chipping, such as sawdust and veneer clippings.

Forest land. Land at least 10 percent stocked with trees of any size, or formerly having had such tree cover, and not currently developed for nonforest use. (Note: Stocking is measured by comparing specified standards with basal area and/or number of trees, age or size, and spacing.) The minimum area for classification of forest land is 1 acre. Roadside, streamside, and shelterbelt strips of timber must have a crown width of at least 120 feet to qualify as forest land. Unimproved roads and trails, streams or other bodies of water, or clearings in forest areas are classified as forest if less than 120 feet wide.

Growing-stock removals. The growing-stock volume removed from timberland by harvesting industrial roundwood products. (Note: Includes sawtimber removals, poletimber removals, and logging residues.)

Growing-stock tree. A live timberland tree of commercial species that meets specified standards of size, quality, and merchantability. (Note: Excludes rough, rotten, and dead trees.)

Growing-stock volume. Net volume of growing-stock trees 5.0 inches d.b.h. and larger, from 1 foot above the ground to a minimum 4.0-inch top diameter outside bark of the central stem or to the point where the central stem breaks into limbs.

Hardwoods. Dicotyledonous trees, usually broad-leaved and deciduous.

Harvest residues. The total net volume of unused portions of trees cut or killed by logging. (Note: Includes both logging residues and logging slash.)

Industrial fuelwood. A roundwood product, with or without bark, used to generate energy at manufacturing facilities and schools, correctional institutions, or electric generating plants.

Imports. The volume of roundwood delivered to a mill or group of mills in a specific state but harvested outside that state.

Industrial roundwood exports. The quantity of industrial roundwood harvested in a geographical area and transported to other geographical areas.

Industrial roundwood imports. The quantity of industrial roundwood received from other geographical areas.

Industrial roundwood products. Saw logs, pulpwood, veneer logs, poles, commercial posts, pilings, cooperage logs, particleboard bolts, shaving bolts, lath bolts, charcoal bolts, and chips from roundwood used for pulp or board products.

Industrial roundwood production. The quantity of industrial roundwood harvested in a geographic area plus all industrial roundwood exported to other geographical areas.

Industrial roundwood receipts. The quantity of industrial roundwood received by commercial mills in a geographic area plus all industrial roundwood imported from other geographical areas.

Industrial roundwood retained. The quantity of industrial roundwood harvested from and processed by commercial mills within the same geographical area.

International ¼-inch rule. A log rule or formula for estimating the board-foot volume of logs, allowing ½ inch of taper for each 4-foot length and assuming ¼ inch of kerf. This rule is used as the U.S. Forest Service standard log rule in the eastern United States.

Limbwood removals. Net volume of all portions of a tree other than the central stem (including forks, large limbs, tops, and stumps) harvested for industrial roundwood products.

Logging residue. The net volume of unused portions of the merchantable central stem of growing-stock trees cut or killed by logging.

Logging slash. The net volume of unused portions of the unmerchantable (non-growing stock) sections of trees cut or killed by logging.

Merchantable sections. Refers to sections of the central stem of growing-stock trees that meet either pulpwood or saw log specifications.

Net volume. Gross volume less deductions for rot, sweep, or other defects affecting use for roundwood products.

Noncommercial species. Trees species of typically small size, poor form, or inferior quality that normally do not develop into trees suitable for industrial roundwood products. Noncommercial species are listed in the volume tables as rough trees.

Nonforest land. Land that has never supported forests, and land formerly forested where use for timber management is precluded by development for other uses. (Note: Includes areas used for crops, active Christmas tree plantations, orchards, nurseries, improved pasture, residential areas, city parks, improved roads of any width and adjoining clearings, powerline clearings of any width, and 1- to 39.9-acre areas of water classified by the Bureau of the Census as land.) If intermingled in forest areas, unimproved roads and nonforest strips must be more than 120 feet wide and more than 1 acre to qualify as nonforest land.

Nonforest land removals. Net volume of trees on nonforest lands harvested for industrial roundwood products.

Poletimber. A growing-stock tree at least 5.0 inches d.b.h. but smaller than sawtimber size (9.0 inches d.b.h. for softwoods, 11.0 inches d.b.h. for hardwoods).

Poletimber removals. Net volume in the merchantable central stem of poletimber trees harvested for industrial roundwood products.

Primary wood-using mills. Mills receiving roundwood or chips from roundwood for processing into products such as lumber, veneer, and pulp.

Primary wood-using mill residue. Wood materials (coarse and fine) and bark generated at manufacturing plants that process industrial roundwood into principal products. These residues include wood products obtained incidental to production of principal products and wood materials not utilized for some product.

Production. The quantity of roundwood material harvested in a geographic area plus all roundwood material exported to other geographical areas.

Receipts. The quantity of roundwood material received by commercial mills in a geographic area plus all roundwood material imported from other geographical areas.

Retained. Roundwood volume harvested from and processed by mills within the same state.

Rotten tree. A tree that does not meet regional merchantability standards because of excessive unsound cull.

Rough tree. A tree that does not meet regional merchantability standards because of excessive sound cull (includes forks, sweep and crook, and large branches or knots), including noncommercial tree species.

Roundwood. Logs, bolts, or other round sections cut from trees (including chips from roundwood).

Sapling. A live tree between 1.0 and 5.0 inches d.b.h.

Saw log portion. That portion of the central stem of sawtimber trees between the stump and the saw log top.

Saw log top. The point on the central stem of sawtimber trees above which a saw log cannot be produced. The minimum saw log top is 7.0 inches diameter outside bark for softwoods and 9.0 inches diameter outside bark for hardwoods.

Sawtimber removals. As used in Table 10, sawtimber removals refers to the net volume in the merchantable central stem of sawtimber-size trees harvested for industrial roundwood products. (Note: includes the saw log and upper stem portions of sawtimber-size trees.) When referring to the sawtimber volume removed from timberland as in Table 12, sawtimber removals refers to the net volume in the saw log portion of sawtimber-size trees harvested for roundwood products or left on the ground as harvest residue, and is usually expressed in thousands of board feet (International ¼-inch rule).

Sawtimber tree. A growing-stock tree containing at least a 12-foot saw log or two noncontiguous saw logs 8 feet or longer, and meeting regional specifications for freedom from defect. Softwoods must be at least 9.0 inches d.b.h. and hardwoods must be at least 11.0 inches d.b.h.

Sawtimber volume. Net volume in the saw log portion of sawtimber trees.

Softwoods. Coniferous trees, usually evergreen, having needles or scale-like leaves.

Timber product output. The volume of roundwood products produced from an area's forests.

Timberland. Forest land that is producing, or is capable of producing, in excess of 20 cubic feet per acre per year of industrial roundwood products under natural conditions, is not withdrawn from timber utilization by statute or administrative regulation, and is not associated with urban or rural development.

Tree. A woody perennial plant, typically large, with a single well-defined stem carrying a more or less definite crown; sometimes defined as attaining a minimum diameter of 3 in. (7.6 cm) and a minimum height of 15 ft (4.6 m) at maturity. For FIA, any plant on the tree list in the current field manual is measured as a tree.

Upper stem portion. That portion of the central stem of sawtimber trees between the saw log top and the minimum top diameter of 4.0 inches outside bark, or to the point where the central stem breaks into limbs.

Common and Scientific Names of Tree Species in this Report

Softwoods

Cedars

Northern white-cedar	*Thuja occidentalis*
Eastern redcedar	*Juniperus virginiana*

Pine

Jack pine	*Pinus banksiana*
Red pine	*Pinus resinosa*
Eastern white pine	*Pinus strobus*

Spruce

White spruce	*Picea glauca*
Black spruce	*Picea mariana*
Balsam fir	*Abies balsamea*
Eastern hemlock	*Tsuga canadensis*
Tamarack	*Larix laricina*

Hardwoods

Ash

    White ash   *Fraxinus americana*

    Black ash   *Fraxinus nigra*

    Green ash   *Fraxinus pennsylvanica*

Aspen/balsam poplar

    Bigtooth aspen   *Populus grandidentata*

    Quaking aspen   *Populus tremuloides*

    Balsam poplar   *Populus balsamifera*

American basswood   *Tilia americana*

American beech   *Fagus grandifolia*

Birch

    River birch   *Betula nigra*

    White birch   *Betula papyrifera*

    Yellow birch   *Betula alleghaniensis*

Black cherry   *Prunus serotina*

Black walnut   *Juglans nigra*

Elm

    American elm   *Ulmus americana*

    Rock elm   *Ulmus thomasii*

    Slippery elm   *Ulmus rubra*

Hickory

    Bitternut hickory   *Carya cordiformis*

    Pignut hickory   *Carya glabra*

    Shagbark hickory   *Carya ovata*

Hard maples

    Black maple   *Acer nigrum*

    Sugar maple   *Acer saccharum*

Soft maples

    Boxelder   *Acer negundo*

    Red maple   *Acer rubrum*

    Silver maple   *Acer saccharinum*

Red oak group

    Northern pin oak   *Quercus ellipsoidalis*

    Northern red oak   *Quercus rubra*

    Black oak   *Quercus velutina*

White oak group

    White oak   *Quercus alba*

    Swamp white oak   *Quercus bicolor*

    Bur oak   *Quercus macrocarpa*

    Chinkapin oak   *Quercus muehlenbergii*

Other hardwoods

    Northern catalpa   *Catalpa speciosa*

    Hackberry   *Celtis occidentalis*

    Honeylocust   *Gleditsia triacanthos*

    Butternut   *Juglans cinerea*

    Black willow   *Salix nigra*

Tables

Table 1.–Conversion factors from reported unit of measure to standard unit of measure (This table is in the Study Methods section.)

Table 2.–Number of active primary wood-using mills by mill type and survey year, Minnesota

Table 3.–Industrial roundwood receipts, in million cubic feet, by mill type, hardwoods and softwoods, and survey year, Minnesota

Table 4.–Industrial roundwood receipts, in thousand cubic feet, by Forest Inventory Unit, species group, and State of origin, Minnesota, 2007

Table 5.–Industrial roundwood production, in million cubic feet, by product, hardwoods and softwoods, and survey year, Minnesota

Table 6.–Industrial roundwood production, in thousand cubic feet, by Forest Inventory Unit, species group, and State of destination, Minnesota, 2007

Table 7.–Industrial roundwood production, in thousand cubic feet, by Forest Inventory Unit, county, and species group, Minnesota, 2007

Table 8.–Industrial roundwood production by Forest Inventory Unit, species group, and product, Minnesota, 2007

Table 9.–Saw log receipts and production, in thousand board feet, International ¼-inch rule, by Forest Inventory Unit and species group, Minnesota, 2004 and 2007

Table 10.–Wood material harvested for industrial roundwood, in thousand cubic feet, by Forest Inventory Unit, source of material, and species group, Minnesota, 2007

Table 11.–Growing-stock removals from timberland for industrial roundwood, in thousand cubic feet, by Forest Inventory Unit, county, and species group, Minnesota, 2007

Table 12.–Sawtimber removals from timberland for industrial roundwood, in thousand board feet, International ¼-inch rule, by Forest Inventory Unit, county, and species group, Minnesota, 2007

Table 13.–Harvest residue generated by industrial roundwood harvesting, in thousand cubic feet, by Forest Inventory Unit, county, and species group, Minnesota, 2007

Table 14.–Disposition of residues produced at primary wood-using mills, in thousand tons, green weight, by Forest Inventory Unit, disposition, residue type, and softwoods and hardwoods, Minnesota, 2007

Table 2.—Number of active primary wood-using mills by mill type and survey year, Minnesota[a]

Kind of mill and mill size		Survey Year							
		1975	1988	1990	1992	1997	2001	2004	2007
Sawmills	Large[b]	9	14	17	15	12	12	9	7
	Medium[c]	29	57	52	43	46	34	25	18
	Small[d]	583	602	447	508	298	291	333	343
	Total	620	673	516	566	356	337	367	368
Veneer mills		4	4	1	1	8	3	2	2
Pulp and composite product mills		9	15	15	16	16	14	14	13
Other products[e]		17	37	19	13	13	13	29	34
All mills		650	729	551	596	393	367	412	417

[a] Mills that produce more than one product are only counted for the product they process the most.

[b] Annual lumber production in excess of 5 million board feet.

[c] Annual lumber production from 1 million to 5 million board feet.

[d] Annual lumber production less than 1 million board feet.

[e] Includes plants producing cabin logs, cooperage, excelsior, shavings, post and poles, etc.

Table 3.—Industrial roundwood receipts, in million cubic feet, by mill type, hardwoods and softwoods, and survey year, Minnesota

Kind of mill	Survey Year								% change from 2004 - 2007
	1975	1988	1990	1992	1997	2001	2004	2007	
All Species									
Saw logs	30.9	55.7	47.3	60.1	56.3	52.2	45.5	43.9	-4%
Pulp mills and composite panels	83.8	156.4	179.1	198.0	216.1	244.1	266.6	178.6	-33%
Other products[a]	6.6	6.4	7.9	6.0	5.5	2.9	6.3	7.3	16%
Total	121.3	218.5	234.3	264.1	277.9	299.2	318.2	229.8	-28%
Softwoods									
Saw logs	9.7	22.4	14.8	27.6	27.6	28.1	29.4	28.3	-4%
Pulp mills and composite panels	28.8	33.3	41.1	33.9	30.9	38.3	45.9	37.7	-18%
Other products[a]	0.3	0.9	2.5	1.5	2.2	1.0	2.3	2.5	9%
Total	38.8	56.6	58.4	63.0	60.7	67.4	77.6	68.6	-12%
Hardwoods									
Saw logs	21.2	33.3	32.5	32.5	28.7	24.1	16.0	15.6	-3%
Pulp mills and composite panels	55.0	123.1	138.0	164.1	185.2	205.8	220.7	140.9	-36%
Other products[a]	6.3	5.5	5.4	4.6	3.2	1.9	4.0	4.8	20%
Total	82.5	161.9	175.9	201.1	217.3	238.8	240.7	161.2	-33%

[a] Includes plants producing veneer, cooperage, cabin logs, post and poles, etc.

Columns and rows may not add to their totals due to rounding.

Table 4.—Industrial roundwood receipts, in thousand cubic feet, by Forest Inventory Unit, species group, and State of origin, Minnesota, 2007

Species group	Total	State of origin								
		Illinois	Iowa	Michigan	Minnesota	North Dakota	South Dakota	Wisconsin	Other States	Canada
ALL UNITS										
Softwoods										
Eastern redcedar	62	--	--	--	31	--	--	0	--	30
Northern white-cedar	932	--	--	--	930	--	--	2	--	1
Cypress	1	--	--	--	--	--	--	--	1	--
Balsam fir	14,791	--	--	--	13,229	--	--	1,509	--	53
Hemlock	0	--	--	--	--	--	--	0	--	--
Jack pine	14,749	--	--	0	12,966	--	--	1,050	--	733
Red pine	16,319	--	--	0	14,556	--	--	1,626	--	137
White pine	1,030	--	--	--	908	--	--	69	--	54
Other pines	466	--	--	--	362	--	--	103	--	1
Spruce	15,954	--	--	--	15,475	--	--	113	--	366
Tamarack	4,249	--	--	0	4,161	--	--	23	--	65
Softwood total	68,553	--	--	1	62,616	--	--	4,496	1	1,439
Hardwoods										
Ash	2,503	--	1	--	2,353	1	1	96	--	52
Aspen/balsam poplar	122,056	--	0	2	112,266	138	--	4,377	--	5,272
Basswood	2,440	--	5	--	2,340	--	--	84	--	11
White birch	13,468	--	0	0	12,668	--	--	571	--	228
Yellow birch	107	--	--	--	93	--	--	0	--	14
Black cherry	14	2	0	--	12	--	--	1	--	1
Black walnut	237	--	34	--	202	--	0	1	--	--

23

Table 4.—Continued

		State of origin								
	Total	Illinois	Iowa	Michigan	Minnesota	North Dakota	South Dakota	Wisconsin	Other States	Canada
Species group										
Cottonwood	1,377	--	1	--	1,289	77	2	4	--	3
Elm	118	--	2	--	115	--	0	1	--	--
Hickory	36	1	0	--	34	--	--	0	--	--
Hard maple	3,259	--	23	--	2,090	--	0	1,123	--	23
Soft maple	9,573	--	2	25	6,094	--	0	3,427	--	26
Red oak group	4,443	--	17	--	4,395	--	--	30	--	--
White oak group	1,500	--	100	--	1,236	1	0	163	--	--
Other hardwoods	94	--	1	--	40	--	--	1	--	52
Hardwood total	161,226	3	186	28	145,227	217	4	9,881	--	5,681
State total	229,779	3	186	28	207,843	217	4	14,377	1	7,120

ASPEN-BIRCH UNIT

Softwoods										
Northern white-cedar	859	--	--	--	856	--	--	2	--	1
Balsam fir	6,157	--	--	--	5,493	--	--	610	--	53
Hemlock	0	--	--	--	--	--	--	0	--	--
Jack pine	3,724	--	--	0	3,205	--	--	381	--	138
Red pine	4,660	--	--	0	3,262	--	--	1,288	--	109
White pine	407	--	--	--	288	--	--	65	--	54
Other pines	458	--	--	--	355	--	--	103	--	0
Spruce	8,178	--	--	--	7,855	--	--	88	--	235
Tamarack	2,917	--	--	0	2,837	--	--	23	--	57
Softwood total	27,359	--	--	1	24,151	--	--	2,561	--	647

Table 4.—Continued

Species group	State of origin									
	Total	Illinois	Iowa	Michigan	Minnesota	North Dakota	South Dakota	Wisconsin	Other States	Canada
Hardwoods										
Ash	1,439	—	—	—	1,317	—	—	73	—	49
Aspen/balsam poplar	66,515	—	—	2	57,666	35	—	3,976	—	4,836
Basswood	547	—	—	—	466	—	—	79	—	2
White birch	9,143	—	—	0	8,383	—	—	571	—	189
Yellow birch	101	—	—	—	87	—	—	0	—	14
Black cherry	0	—	—	—	0	—	—	0	—	—
Black walnut	0	—	—	—	—	—	—	0	—	—
Cottonwood	0	—	—	—	0	—	—	—	—	—
Elm	1	—	—	—	1	—	—	0	—	—
Hickory	0	—	—	—	0	—	—	0	—	—
Hard maple	2,051	—	—	—	911	—	—	1,121	—	18
Soft maple	8,702	—	—	25	5,234	—	—	3,424	—	20
Red oak group	33	—	—	—	29	—	—	4	—	—
White oak group	15	—	—	—	14	—	—	1	—	—
Other hardwoods	53	—	—	—	0	—	—	0	—	52
Hardwood total	88,600	—	—	28	74,108	35	—	9,248	—	5,182
Unit total	115,960	—	—	28	98,259	35	—	11,809	—	5,829
CENTRAL HARDWOODS UNIT										
Softwoods										
Eastern redcedar	57	—	—	—	27	—	—	0	—	30
Northern white-cedar	0	—	—	—	0	—	—	—	—	—

Table 4.—Continued

Species group	Total	Illinois	Iowa	Michigan	Minnesota	North Dakota	South Dakota	Wisconsin	Other States	Canada
								State of origin		
Balsam fir	4,698	--	--	--	3,851	--	--	848	--	--
Jack pine	252	--	--	--	250	--	--	2	--	--
Red pine	473	--	--	--	469	--	--	4	--	--
White pine	128	--	--	--	125	--	--	4	--	--
Other pines	2	--	--	--	2	--	--	0	--	--
Spruce	1,539	--	--	--	1,519	--	--	20	--	--
Tamarack	7	--	--	--	7	--	--	--	--	--
Softwood total	7,158	--	--	--	6,250	--	--	878	--	30
Hardwoods										
Ash	325	--	0	--	301	--	--	24	--	--
Aspen/balsam poplar	7,461	--	0	--	7,155	--	--	306	--	--
Basswood	439	--	0	--	433	--	--	5	--	--
White birch	61	--	0	--	60	--	--	1	--	--
Yellow birch	0	--	--	--	0	--	--	--	--	--
Black cherry	12	2	0	--	10	--	--	1	--	--
Black walnut	46	--	0	--	44	--	--	1	--	--
Cottonwood	722	--	0	--	695	22	--	4	--	--
Elm	95	--	0	--	94	--	--	1	--	--
Hickory	35	1	0	--	33	--	--	0	--	--
Hard maple	284	--	22	--	259	--	--	2	--	--
Soft maple	102	--	0	--	98	--	--	3	--	--
Red oak group	2,240	--	17	--	2,197	--	--	27	--	--

Table 4.—Continued

| | | State of origin | | | | | | | | |
Species group	Total	Illinois	Iowa	Michigan	Minnesota	North Dakota	South Dakota	Wisconsin	Other States	Canada
White oak group	1,130	--	97	--	871	--	--	162	--	--
Other hardwoods	29	--	0	--	29	--	--	1	--	--
Hardwood total	12,979	3	138	--	12,280	22	--	537	--	--
Unit total	20,137	3	138	--	18,529	22	--	1,415	--	30

NORTHERN PINE UNIT

Species group	Total	Illinois	Iowa	Michigan	Minnesota	North Dakota	South Dakota	Wisconsin	Other States	Canada
Softwoods										
Northern white-cedar	72	--	--	--	72	--	--	--	--	--
Cypress	1	--	--	--	--	--	--	--	1	--
Balsam fir	3,935	--	--	--	3,884	--	--	51	--	0
Jack pine	10,772	--	--	--	9,509	--	--	667	--	595
Red pine	11,183	--	--	--	10,822	--	--	334	--	28
White pine	494	--	--	--	494	--	--	--	--	0
Other pines	5	--	--	--	5	--	--	--	--	0
Spruce	6,231	--	--	--	6,096	--	--	5	--	131
Tamarack	1,240	--	--	--	1,233	--	--	--	--	8
Softwood total	33,934	--	--	--	32,114	--	--	1,057	1	762
Hardwoods										
Ash	558	--	--	--	556	0	--	--	--	2
Aspen/balsam poplar	48,057	--	--	--	47,422	103	--	96	--	436
Basswood	1,265	--	--	--	1,256	--	--	--	--	9
White birch	4,262	--	--	--	4,223	--	--	--	--	39
Yellow birch	6	--	--	--	6	--	--	--	--	--

Table 4.—Continued

| | | State of origin | | | | | | | Other | |
Species group	Total	Illinois	Iowa	Michigan	Minnesota	North Dakota	South Dakota	Wisconsin	States	Canada
Black cherry	0	--	--	--	0	--	--	--	--	--
Cottonwood	335	--	--	--	278	55	--	--	--	3
Elm	1	--	--	--	1	--	--	--	--	--
Hard maple	908	--	--	--	903	--	--	--	--	5
Soft maple	741	--	--	--	736	--	--	--	--	5
Red oak group	2,086	--	--	--	2,086	--	--	--	--	--
White oak group	275	--	--	--	274	1	--	--	--	--
Other hardwoods	4	--	--	--	4	--	--	--	--	--
Hardwood total	58,499	--	--	--	57,744	159	--	96	--	499
Unit total	92,433	--	--	--	89,859	159	--	1,152	1	1,261

PRAIRIE UNIT

Softwoods										
Eastern redcedar	4	--	--	--	4	--	--	--	--	--
Northern white-cedar	1	--	--	--	1	--	--	--	--	--
Balsam fir	1	--	--	--	1	--	--	--	--	--
Jack pine	2	--	--	--	2	--	--	--	--	--
Red pine	3	--	--	--	3	--	--	--	--	--
White pine	2	--	--	--	2	--	--	--	--	--
Other pines	0	--	--	--	0	--	--	--	--	--
Spruce	5	--	--	--	5	--	--	--	--	--
Tamarack	84	--	--	--	84	--	--	--	--	--
Softwood total	102	--	--	--	102	--	--	--	--	--

Table 4.—Continued

| | | State of origin | | | | | | | | |
Species group	Total	Illinois	Iowa	Michigan	Minnesota	North Dakota	South Dakota	Wisconsin	Other States	Canada
Hardwoods										
Ash	181	--	1	--	179	0	1	--	--	--
Aspen/balsam poplar	23	--	--	--	23	--	--	--	--	--
Basswood	189	--	5	--	185	--	--	--	--	--
White birch	3	--	--	--	3	--	--	--	--	--
Yellow birch	0	--	--	--	0	--	--	--	--	--
Black cherry	2	--	--	--	2	--	--	--	--	--
Black walnut	192	--	34	--	158	--	0	--	--	--
Cottonwood	320	--	1	--	316	1	2	--	--	--
Elm	21	--	1	--	20	--	0	--	--	--
Hickory	1	--	0	--	1	--	--	--	--	--
Hard maple	17	--	0	--	16	--	0	--	--	--
Soft maple	28	--	2	--	26	--	0	--	--	--
Red oak group	83	--	0	--	83	--	0	--	--	--
White oak group	80	--	3	--	77	--	0	--	--	--
Other hardwoods	8	--	1	--	7	--	--	--	--	--
Hardwood total	1,148	--	48	--	1,094	1	4	--	--	--
Unit total	1,250	--	48	--	1,196	1	4	--	--	--

All table cells without observations are indicated by -- . Table value of 0 indicates the volume rounds to less than 1 thousand cubic feet. Columns and rows may not add to their totals due to rounding.

Table 5.—Industrial roundwood production, in million cubic feet, by product, hardwoods and softwoods, and survey year, Minnesota

Product	Survey Year								% change from 2004 - 2007
	1975	1988	1990	1992	1997	2001	2004	2007	
All Species									
Saw logs	28.2	55.1	47.3	58.7	54.2	55.5	47.3	42.3	-11%
Veneer logs	0.5	2.6	2.7	2.8	2.1	1.7	1.3	1.4	13%
Pulp and composite products	98.8	158.7	179.1	203.4	226.2	216.7	226.2	166.8	-26%
Industrial fuelwood	--	0.7	0.7	0.8	--	--	--	3.6	--
Poles	0.6	0.4	0.4	0.5	1.7	0.3	0.3	0.4	23%
Posts	1.4	2.6	0.5	0.9	0.1	0.2	--	0.2	--
Other products[a]	6.1	3.7	3.7	2.0	0.5	0.7	0.3	2.3	582%
Total	135.7	223.8	234.4	269.0	284.8	275.1	275.4	217.0	-21%
Softwoods									
Saw logs	11.3	20.8	14.8	23.4	22.9	27.0	27.8	25.2	-10%
Veneer logs	--	0.0	0.0	--	--	--	--	--	--
Pulp and composite products	45.7	35.2	41.1	37.0	40.1	43.4	45.2	37.0	-18%
Industrial fuelwood	--	--	--	--	--	--	--	0.9	--
Poles	0.6	0.4	0.4	0.5	1.7	0.3	0.3	0.4	23%
Posts	1.4	2.6	0.5	0.9	0.1	0.2	--	0.2	--
Other products[a]	0.2	0.9	1.7	0.5	0.2	0.0	0.2	1.5	792%
Total	59.2	59.8	58.4	62.3	64.9	70.9	73.5	65.2	-11%
Hardwoods									
Saw logs	17.0	34.4	32.5	35.2	31.3	28.5	19.5	17.1	-12%
Veneer logs	0.5	2.6	2.7	2.8	2.1	1.7	1.3	1.4	13%
Pulp and composite products	53.2	123.5	138.0	166.4	186.2	173.3	181.0	129.7	-28%
Industrial fuelwood	--	0.7	0.7	0.8	--	--	--	2.7	--

Table 5.—Continued

| Product | Survey Year | | | | | | | | | % change from |
	1975	1988	1990	1992	1997	2001	2004	2007		2004 - 2007
Poles	--	--	--	--	--	--	--			--
Posts	--	--	--	--	--	--	--	0.0		--
Other products[a]	5.9	2.8	2.0	1.5	0.4	0.6	0.2	0.8		374%
Total	76.6	164.0	176.0	206.8	219.9	204.2	201.9	151.8		-25%

[a] Includes plants producing handles, excelsior, shavings, cabin logs, etc.

All table cells without observations are indicated by -- . Table value of 0.0 indicates the volume rounds to less than 1 million cubic feet. Columns and rows may not add to their totals due to rounding.

Table 6.—Industrial roundwood production, in thousand cubic feet, by Forest Inventory Unit, species group, and State of destination, Minnesota, 2007

Species group	Total	Indiana	Iowa	Michigan	Minnesota	Ohio	South Dakota	Wisconsin	Canada	Other countries
					ALL UNITS					
Softwoods										
Eastern redcedar	31	--	--	--	31	--	--	--	--	--
Northern white-cedar	930	--	--	--	930	--	--	--	--	--
Balsam fir	13,252	--	--	--	13,229	--	--	--	23	--
Jack pine	13,135	--	--	--	12,966	--	--	--	169	--
Red pine	14,813	--	--	33	14,556	--	--	160	65	--
White pine	916	--	--	--	908	--	--	9	--	--
Other pines	362	--	--	--	362	--	--	--	--	--
Spruce	17,465	--	--	--	15,475	--	--	1,789	201	--
Tamarack	4,256	--	--	--	4,161	--	--	--	95	--
Softwood total	65,160	--	--	33	62,616	--	--	1,958	553	--
Hardwoods										
Ash	2,399	0	3	--	2,353	0	0	34	--	9
Aspen/balsam poplar	113,922	--	12	16	112,266	--	--	1,626	2	--
Basswood	2,473	--	11	--	2,340	--	--	105	--	17
Beech	14	--	--	--	--	--	--	14	--	--
White birch	14,362	--	--	--	12,668	--	--	1,692	0	1
Yellow birch	137	--	--	--	93	--	--	44	--	--
Black cherry	59	0	11	--	12	14	--	22	--	0
Black walnut	360	17	4	--	202	7	1	54	--	76
Cottonwood	1,320	--	27	--	1,289	--	4	0	--	--

Table 6.—Continued

| | | State of destiniation | | | | | South | | | Other |
Species group	Total	Indiana	Iowa	Michigan	Minnesota	Ohio	Dakota	Wisconsin	Canada	countries
Elm	143	–	7	–	115	–	0	12	–	8
Hickory	80	0	15	–	34	–	–	31	–	0
Hard maple	2,702	0	19	–	2,090	30	–	536	–	28
Soft maple	6,152	–	17	–	6,094	–	–	42	–	–
Red oak group	6,017	–	478	–	4,395	–	–	1,140	–	4
White oak group	1,608	–	157	–	1,236	–	–	201	–	13
Other hardwoods	42	–	–	–	40	–	–	2	–	–
Hardwood total	151,792	18	762	16	145,227	51	5	5,554	3	156
State total	216,951	18	762	49	207,843	51	5	7,511	556	156

ASPEN-BIRCH UNIT

Species group	Total	Indiana	Iowa	Michigan	Minnesota	Ohio	Dakota	Wisconsin	Canada	countries
Softwoods										
Northern white-cedar	860	–	–	–	860	–	–	–	–	–
Balsam fir	7,239	–	–	–	7,216	–	–	–	23	–
Jack pine	3,764	–	–	–	3,595	–	–	–	169	–
Red pine	4,772	–	–	–	4,677	–	–	31	65	–
White pine	291	–	–	–	291	–	–	–	–	–
Other pines	217	–	–	–	217	–	–	–	–	–
Spruce	11,650	–	–	–	9,897	–	–	1,552	201	–
Tamarack	1,983	–	–	–	1,888	–	–	–	95	–
Softwood total	30,777	–	–	–	28,641	–	–	1,583	553	–
Hardwoods										
Ash	1,066	0	–	–	1,065	0	–	–	–	1

Table 6.—Continued

Species group	Total				State of destiniation		South			Other
		Indiana	Iowa	Michigan	Minnesota	Ohio	Dakota	Wisconsin	Canada	countries
Aspen/balsam poplar	38,589	—	—	11	38,469	—	—	107	2	—
Basswood	276	—	—	—	276	—	—	—	—	—
White birch	6,911	—	—	—	5,800	—	—	1,110	0	—
Yellow birch	65	—	—	—	65	—	—	—	—	—
Cottonwood	6	—	—	—	6	—	—	—	—	—
Elm	1	—	—	—	1	—	—	—	—	—
Hard maple	808	0	—	—	671	3	—	133	—	0
Soft maple	1,797	—	—	—	1,797	—	—	—	—	—
Red oak group	95	—	—	—	82	—	—	13	—	—
White oak group	21	—	—	—	12	—	—	9	—	—
Other hardwoods	0	—	—	—	0	—	—	—	—	—
Hardwood total	49,635	0	—	11	48,245	3	—	1,373	2	1
Unit total	80,411	0	—	11	76,886	3	—	2,956	555	1
CENTRAL HARDWOODS UNIT										
Softwoods										
Eastern redcedar	27	—	—	—	27	—	—	—	—	—
Balsam fir	115	—	—	—	115	—	—	—	—	—
Jack pine	496	—	—	—	496	—	—	—	—	—
Red pine	808	—	—	33	699	—	—	76	—	—
White pine	109	—	—	—	101	—	—	9	—	—
Other pines	81	—	—	—	81	—	—	—	—	—
Spruce	41	—	—	—	41	—	—	—	—	—

34

Table 6.—Continued

Species group	Total	State of destiniation					South Dakota	Wisconsin	Canada	Other countries
		Indiana	Iowa	Michigan	Minnesota	Ohio				
Tamarack	71	--	--	--	71	--	--	--	--	--
Softwood total	1,751	--	--	33	1,633	--	--	85	--	--
Hardwoods										
Ash	444	0	3	--	407	0	--	33	--	1
Aspen/balsam poplar	10,647	--	12	1	9,353	--	--	1,282	--	--
Basswood	577	--	11	--	467	--	--	99	--	--
White birch	745	--	--	--	576	--	--	169	--	--
Yellow birch	29	--	--	--	0	--	--	28	--	--
Beech	14	--	--	--	--	--	--	14	--	--
Black cherry	54	0	11	--	9	14	--	19	--	0
Black walnut	231	13	4	--	136	5	--	45	--	28
Cottonwood	695	--	27	--	668	--	--	0	--	--
Elm	118	--	7	--	93	--	--	12	--	6
Hickory	76	0	15	--	31	--	--	30	--	0
Hard maple	746	0	19	--	449	16	--	255	--	8
Soft maple	1,360	--	17	--	1,305	--	--	38	--	--
Red oak group	3,554	--	478	--	2,041	--	--	1,036	--	--
White oak group	1,256	--	157	--	900	--	--	192	--	6
Other hardwoods	31	--	--	--	29	--	--	2	--	--
Hardwood total	20,578	14	762	1	16,464	35	--	3,253	--	49
Unit total	22,328	14	762	34	18,096	35	--	3,338	--	49

Table 6.—Continued

| | | | | | State of destiniation | | South | | | Other |
Species group	Total	Indiana	Iowa	Michigan	Minnesota	Ohio	Dakota	Wisconsin	Canada	countries
					NORTHERN PINE UNIT					
Softwoods										
Northern white-cedar	70	–	–	–	70	–	–	–	–	–
Balsam fir	5,893	–	–	–	5,893	–	–	–	0	–
Jack pine	8,847	–	–	–	8,847	–	–	–	–	–
Red pine	9,216	–	–	–	9,163	–	–	53	–	–
White pine	515	–	–	–	515	–	–	–	–	–
Other pines	63	–	–	–	63	–	–	–	–	–
Spruce	5,770	–	–	–	5,533	–	–	237	–	–
Tamarack	2,194	–	–	–	2,194	–	–	–	–	–
Softwood total	32,568	–	–	–	32,278	–	–	290	0	–
Hardwoods										
Ash	792	0	–	–	784	0	–	1	–	7
Aspen/balsam poplar	62,612	–	–	5	62,370	–	–	236	1	–
Basswood	1,460	–	–	–	1,454	–	–	6	–	1
White birch	6,670	–	–	–	6,257	–	–	413	0	1
Yellow birch	43	–	–	–	27	–	–	15	–	–
Black cherry	3	–	–	–	0	–	–	3	–	–
Black walnut	9	–	–	–	–	–	–	9	–	–
Cottonwood	74	–	–	–	74	–	–	–	–	–
Elm	1	–	–	–	1	–	–	–	–	–
Hickory	1	–	–	–	–	–	–	1	–	–

Table 6.—Continued

| | | State of destination | | | | | | South | | | Other |
Species group	Total	Indiana	Iowa	Michigan	Minnesota	Ohio	Dakota	Wisconsin	Canada	countries
Hard maple	1,095	0	—	—	940	7	—	148	—	1
Soft maple	2,971	—	—	—	2,968	—	—	3	—	—
Red oak group	2,219	—	—	—	2,128	—	—	91	—	—
White oak group	233	—	—	—	232	—	—	1	—	—
Other hardwoods	4	—	—	—	4	—	—	—	—	—
Hardwood total	78,190	0	—	5	77,240	7	—	927	1	9
Unit total	110,758	0	—	5	109,518	7	—	1,217	1	9

PRAIRIE UNIT

Species group	Total	Indiana	Iowa	Michigan	Minnesota	Ohio	Dakota	Wisconsin	Canada	countries
Softwoods										
Eastern redcedar	4	—	—	—	4	—	—	—	—	—
Balsam fir	5	—	—	—	5	—	—	—	—	—
Jack pine	27	—	—	—	27	—	—	—	—	—
Red pine	16	—	—	—	16	—	—	—	—	—
White pine	1	—	—	—	1	—	—	—	—	—
Other pines	0	—	—	—	0	—	—	—	—	—
Spruce	3	—	—	—	3	—	—	—	—	—
Tamarack	7	—	—	—	7	—	—	—	—	—
Softwood total	64	—	—	—	64	—	—	—	—	—
Hardwoods										
Ash	98	0	—	—	97	0	0	—	—	—
Aspen/balsam poplar	2,074	—	—	—	2,074	—	—	—	—	—
Basswood	159	—	—	—	143	—	—	—	—	16

37

Table 6.—Continued

Species group	Total	Indiana	Iowa	Michigan	Minnesota	State of destination Ohio	South Dakota	Wisconsin	Canada	Other countries
White birch	36	--	--	--	36	--	--	--	--	--
Yellow birch	0	--	--	--	0	--	--	--	--	--
Black cherry	2	--	--	--	2	--	--	--	--	--
Black walnut	119	4	--	--	66	2	1	--	--	48
Cottonwood	546	--	--	--	542	--	4	--	--	--
Elm	23	--	--	--	21	--	0	--	--	2
Hickory	3	0	--	--	3	--	--	--	--	--
Hard maple	52	0	--	--	29	4	--	--	--	19
Soft maple	24	--	--	--	24	--	--	--	--	--
Red oak group	148	--	--	--	144	--	--	--	--	4
White oak group	98	--	--	--	91	--	--	--	--	7
Other hardwoods	7	--	--	--	7	--	--	--	--	--
Hardwood total	3,389	4	--	--	3,278	6	5	--	--	97
Unit total	3,454	4	--	--	3,342	6	5	--	--	97

All table cells without observations are indicated by --. Table value of 0 indicates the volume rounds to less than 1 thousand cubic feet. Columns and rows may not add to their totals due to rounding.

Table 7.—Industrial roundwood production, in thousand cubic feet, by Forest Inventory Unit, county, and species group, Minnesota, 2007

Forest Inventory Unit and county	All species	Eastern redcedar	Northern white-cedar	Balsam fir	Jack pine	Red pine	White pine	Other pine	Spruce	Tama-rack	Total softwoods	Ash	Aspen/balsam poplar	Bass-wood
Aspen-Birch Unit														
Carlton	5,119	–	5	353	38	696	8	33	159	48	1,340	214	2,809	28
Cook	2,602	–	2	135	60	461	45	84	646	0	1,434	0	1,014	–
Koochiching	18,743	–	684	1,763	530	603	47	1	4,015	875	8,517	126	9,115	106
Lake	7,018	–	6	833	344	522	28	16	988	83	2,820	116	2,417	49
St. Louis	46,929	–	162	4,154	2,791	2,491	163	83	5,843	977	16,665	610	23,234	93
Total	80,411	–	860	7,239	3,764	4,772	291	217	11,650	1,983	30,777	1,066	38,589	276
Central Hardwoods Unit														
Anoka	109	0	–	–	1	37	6	–	–	1	44	12	15	0
Benton	74	–	–	–	12	19	–	0	0	1	32	0	18	2
Carver	59	1	–	–	–	–	–	–	–	–	1	1	–	–
Chisago	299	0	–	–	0	28	7	0	0	0	36	17	63	7
Dakota	58	–	–	–	2	2	2	–	–	–	6	9	4	0
Douglas	596	–	–	0	241	0	0	–	0	0	242	7	11	21
Fillmore	772	1	–	–	–	1	1	0	1	–	4	27	3	53
Goodhue	503	1	–	–	–	–	0	–	1	–	3	24	41	79
Hennepin	94	5	–	–	–	1	1	–	–	–	6	17	7	2
Houston	1,410	–	–	–	–	0	–	–	–	–	0	17	18	52
Isanti	310	0	–	–	12	14	28	0	0	1	54	20	87	5
Kanabec	1,657	0	–	0	1	18	11	–	1	18	49	25	1,202	63
Le Sueur	58	0	–	–	0	0	0	–	0	–	1	3	–	2

Table 7.—Continued

		Softwoods										Hardwoods		
Forest Inventory Unit and county	All species	Eastern redcedar	Northern white-cedar	Balsam fir	Jack pine	Red pine	White pine	Other pine	Spruce	Tama-rack	Total softwoods	Ash	Aspen/ balsam poplar	Bass-wood
Mille Lacs	1,580	—	—	—	14	10	7	—	0	10	41	20	1,022	46
Morrison	1,988	0	—	—	28	42	5	1	1	5	82	13	1,784	6
Olmsted	261	—	—	—	0	1	0	—	0	—	1	8	1	16
Otter Tail	793	—	—	0	16	15	11	0	0	5	48	12	580	22
Pine	8,645	1	—	112	123	503	5	79	36	25	884	96	5,340	49
Ramsey	37	—	—	—	1	2	1	0	0	—	4	10	6	—
Rice	86	1	—	—	—	—	—	—	—	—	1	4	0	4
Scott	132	2	—	—	—	—	—	—	—	—	2	12	4	2
Sherburne	99	0	—	0	12	24	0	0	0	0	37	19	12	0
Stearns	164	1	—	—	—	27	1	—	0	0	29	12	21	9
Todd	981	9	—	3	34	30	4	0	—	5	84	11	364	56
Wabasha	650	2	—	—	—	13	6	—	1	—	21	9	10	46
Washington	55	0	—	—	—	2	1	—	—	0	4	13	6	0
Winona	752	—	—	—	—	3	11	—	0	—	14	14	24	28
Wright	106	2	—	—	—	17	1	—	—	—	21	11	3	7
Total	22,328	27	—	115	496	808	109	81	41	71	1,751	444	10,647	577
Northern Pine Unit														
Aitkin	13,781	—	2	396	201	393	48	8	462	237	1,748	302	7,669	557
Becker	4,626	—	—	327	311	341	27	9	43	18	1,077	12	2,967	53
Beltrami	17,240	—	27	1,300	815	582	77	1	1,049	461	4,313	55	11,542	97
Cass	14,561	—	3	244	1,759	2,532	183	2	190	178	5,090	94	6,887	250

Table 7.—Continued

Forest Inventory Unit and county	All species	Softwoods										Hardwoods		
		Eastern redcedar	Northern white-cedar	Balsam fir	Jack pine	Red pine	White pine	Other pine	Spruce	Tama-rack	Total softwoods	Ash	Aspen/balsam poplar	Bass-wood
Clearwater	4,948	—	—	241	49	184	62	0	296	78	910	7	3,490	109
Crow Wing	4,986	—	14	37	493	699	25	20	27	21	1,336	34	3,107	48
Hubbard	10,722	—	—	353	1,215	1,622	28	12	159	98	3,486	18	6,282	51
Itasca	28,912	—	23	2,597	1,826	1,820	53	10	2,824	609	9,762	241	15,149	212
Lake of the Woods	4,977	—	2	291	823	216	0	0	508	444	2,285	12	2,457	11
Mahnomen	822	—	—	5	10	26	0	0	0	2	42	5	679	33
Roseau	1,498	—	—	92	293	99	0	0	210	28	723	4	686	13
Wadena	3,685	—	—	10	1,052	702	11	0	3	19	1,796	9	1,699	27
Total	110,758	—	70	5,893	8,847	9,216	515	63	5,770	2,194	32,568	792	62,612	1,460
Prairie Unit														
Big Stone	18	0	—	—	—	—	—	—	—	—	0	0	—	—
Blue Earth	129	1	—	—	—	1	0	—	—	—	2	2	0	1
Brown	96	0	—	—	—	0	—	—	—	—	0	2	—	1
Chippewa	7	0	—	—	—	0	—	—	—	—	0	3	—	—
Clay	43	—	—	—	—	—	—	—	—	—	—	4	0	30
Cottonwood	5	—	—	—	—	0	0	—	0	—	1	1	—	—
Dodge	17	—	—	—	0	0	0	—	0	—	0	0	1	0
Faribault	187	—	—	—	—	—	—	—	1	—	1	8	—	16
Freeborn	70	—	—	—	—	—	—	—	—	—	—	13	—	—
Grant	1	—	—	—	—	—	—	—	—	—	—	—	—	0
Jackson	1	—	—	—	—	—	—	—	0	—	0	0	—	—
Kandiyohi	19	1	—	—	—	—	—	—	—	—	1	7	0	3

Table 7.—Continued

Forest Inventory Unit and county	All species	Softwoods										Hardwoods		
		Eastern redcedar	Northern white-cedar	Balsam fir	Jack pine	Red pine	White pine	Other pine	Spruce	Tama-rack	Total softwoods	Ash	Aspen/balsam poplar	Bass-wood
Kittson	882	—	—	0	8	5	—	0	0	2	15	1	843	3
Lac Qui Parle	9	0	—	—	—	—	—	—	—	—	0	0	—	—
Lincoln	6	—	—	—	—	0	—	—	—	—	0	1	—	—
Lyon	8	—	—	—	—	0	—	—	0	—	0	2	0	—
Marshall	409	—	—	0	10	6	0	0	0	3	19	1	368	3
Martin	1	—	—	—	—	—	—	—	—	—	—	0	—	—
McLeod	3	—	—	—	—	—	—	—	—	—	—	0	0	0
Meeker	12	1	—	—	—	—	—	—	—	—	1	3	0	1
Mower	36	—	—	—	—	—	—	—	—	—	—	7	—	0
Murray	2	—	—	—	—	—	—	—	0	—	0	0	0	—
Nicollet	107	0	—	—	—	—	—	—	—	—	0	2	—	16
Nobles	1	—	—	—	—	—	—	—	0	—	0	0	—	—
Norman	95	—	—	—	2	1	—	—	—	1	4	6	44	31
Pennington	114	—	—	—	2	1	—	—	0	1	4	0	105	1
Pipestone	319	—	—	—	0	—	—	—	—	—	0	1	306	8
Polk	626	—	—	5	3	1	—	—	—	1	10	5	363	31
Pope	10	—	—	—	—	—	—	—	—	—	—	5	0	0
Red Lake	60	—	—	—	1	1	—	—	—	0	3	2	43	4
Redwood	17	—	—	—	—	—	—	—	0	—	0	1	0	—
Renville	15	0	—	—	—	—	—	—	0	—	1	2	0	0
Rock	13	—	—	—	—	—	—	—	—	—	—	3	—	—

Table 7.—Continued

Forest Inventory Unit and county	All species	Softwoods										Hardwoods		
		Eastern redcedar	Northern white-cedar	Balsam fir	Jack pine	Red pine	White pine	Other pine	Spruce	Tama-rack	Total softwoods	Ash	Aspen/balsam poplar	Bass-wood
Sibley	15	0	—	—	—	—	—	—	—	—	0	0	—	0
Steele	64	—	—	—	—	0	—	—	—	—	0	10	0	5
Stevens	0	—	—	—	—	—	—	—	—	—	—	0	—	—
Swift	11	—	—	—	0	—	—	—	—	—	0	5	—	0
Waseca	25	—	—	—	—	—	—	—	0	—	0	0	—	2
Watonwan	1	—	—	—	—	—	—	—	—	—	—	0	—	—
Wilkin	1	—	—	—	—	—	—	—	—	—	—	—	—	1
Total	3,454	4	—	5	27	16	1	0	3	7	64	98	2,074	159
State total	216,951	31	930	13,252	13,135	14,813	916	362	17,465	4,256	65,160	2,399	113,922	2,473

Table 7.—Continued

Forest Inventory Unit and county	Hardwoods (continued)													
	Beech	White birch	Yellow birch	Black cherry	Black walnut	Cotton-wood	Elm	Hickory	Hard maple	Soft maple	Red oak group	White oak group	Other hardwoods	Total hardwoods
Aspen-Birch Unit														
Carlton	–	268	0	–	–	0	0	–	58	312	81	10	0	3,779
Cook	–	152	–	–	–	–	–	–	0	1	–	–	–	1,168
Koochiching	–	777	0	–	–	6	0	–	29	53	3	10	0	10,226
Lake	–	892	1	–	–	0	0	–	119	605	–	0	0	4,198
St. Louis	–	4,821	65	–	–	0	0	–	602	826	12	1	0	30,264
Total	–	6,911	65	–	–	6	1	–	808	1,797	95	21	0	49,635
Central Hardwoods Unit														
Anoka	–	1	0	0	0	0	1	–	0	1	29	4	0	65
Benton	–	1	–	–	–	4	0	–	1	0	7	9	0	42
Carver	–	–	–	–	–	22	0	–	2	0	13	14	6	58
Chisago	4	5	0	0	–	5	2	4	23	3	119	12	0	263
Dakota	–	0	–	1	0	8	1	0	0	2	13	11	0	51
Douglas	–	1	–	–	0	278	4	–	3	1	12	16	0	354
Fillmore	–	0	–	7	41	2	32	10	63	8	341	181	0	769
Goodhue	–	2	–	4	19	3	8	2	37	18	203	59	0	501
Hennepin	–	–	–	1	2	1	1	0	9	0	27	16	4	87
Houston	–	1	–	11	49	11	16	30	62	21	854	267	1	1,410
Isanti	–	95	–	0	0	5	3	0	3	4	25	7	0	255
Kanabec	–	44	11	3	7	0	1	0	43	33	163	12	1	1,608
Le Sueur	–	–	–	1	7	28	1	0	3	1	9	2	0	57

Table 7.—Continued

Forest Inventory Unit and county	Beech	White birch	Yellow birch	Black cherry	Black walnut	Cotton-wood	Elm	Hickory	Hard maple	Soft maple	Red oak group	White oak group	Other hardwoods	Total hardwoods
Mille Lacs	—	26	0	—	—	1	—	—	28	66	241	85	5	1,539
Morrison	—	17	—	—	—	5	0	—	2	22	23	34	—	1,905
Olmsted	—	—	—	5	26	3	8	3	16	6	118	49	0	260
Otter Tail	—	25	—	—	0	2	—	—	13	7	61	24	1	745
Pine	11	483	0	0	0	0	0	11	304	1,101	340	26	0	7,761
Ramsey	—	—	—	—	0	0	0	—	—	—	11	5	—	33
Rice	—	4	7	1	5	2	2	0	24	1	26	6	0	85
Scott	—	0	—	0	1	51	5	—	3	3	22	18	8	129
Sherburne	—	1	—	0	—	1	0	—	1	2	17	9	0	62
Steams	—	1	0	2	4	3	2	1	3	3	53	21	0	135
Todd	—	30	11	2	7	189	3	1	37	9	108	68	—	897
Wabasha	—	2	—	8	23	32	12	4	30	39	267	146	2	629
Washington	—	6	—	1	0	0	0	0	0	1	14	11	0	51
Winona	—	1	—	8	39	18	14	10	32	9	414	126	1	739
Wright	—	0	—	0	—	21	1	—	3	0	22	17	0	86
Total	14	745	29	54	231	695	118	76	746	1,360	3,554	1,256	31	20,578
Northern Pine Unit														
Aitkin	—	1,041	0	0	—	1	1	—	158	1,541	714	48	2	12,034
Becker	—	189	10	2	5	8	0	0	169	49	79	6	1	3,549
Beltrami	—	857	—	—	—	14	0	—	185	75	88	14	1	12,926

Hardwoods (continued)

45

Table 7.—Continued

	Hardwoods (continued)										Red oak	White oak	Other	Total
Forest Inventory Unit and county	Beech	White birch	Yellow birch	Black cherry	Black walnut	Cotton-wood	Elm	Hickory	Hard maple	Soft maple	group	group	hardwoods	hardwoods
Cass	–	865	10	2	5	10	0	0	188	434	627	98	1	9,471
Clearwater	–	280	–	0	–	3	0	–	105	34	8	2	0	4,039
Crow Wing	–	207	0	0	–	4	0	–	11	77	137	25	0	3,650
Hubbard	–	593	–	–	–	11	–	–	65	152	62	–	1	7,236
Itasca	–	2,273	22	–	–	5	0	–	152	573	493	30	0	19,150
Lake of the Woods	–	197	–	–	–	3	0	–	5	6	1	1	0	2,692
Mahnomen	–	16	–	–	–	5	0	–	39	2	0	1	–	780
Roseau	–	55	–	–	–	4	–	–	6	8	–	0	–	775
Wadena	–	98	–	0	–	7	0	–	12	22	10	7	0	1,889
Total	–	6,670	43	3	9	74	1	1	1,095	2,971	2,219	233	4	78,190
Prairie Unit														
Big Stone	–	–	–	–	–	17	0	–	1	–	–	–	–	18
Blue Earth	–	–	–	0	33	70	2	–	1	4	3	9	1	127
Brown	–	–	–	–	22	65	0	–	1	0	3	1	0	95
Chippewa	–	–	–	–	0	4	1	–	–	–	–	0	–	7
Clay	–	–	–	–	–	4	0	–	0	0	–	3	–	43
Cottonwood	–	–	–	–	2	1	–	–	–	–	–	–	–	4
Dodge	–	–	–	0	7	0	2	0	2	1	0	4	0	17
Faribault	–	–	–	0	8	1	8	3	17	–	96	28	–	186
Freeborn	–	–	–	1	–	32	–	–	–	–	14	11	0	70
Grant	–	–	–	–	0	–	–	–	–	–	0	0	–	1

Table 7.—Continued

Forest Inventory Unit and county	Hardwoods (continued)													
	Beech	White birch	Yellow birch	Black cherry	Black walnut	Cotton-wood	Elm	Hickory	Hard maple	Soft maple	Red oak group	White oak group	Other hardwoods	Total hardwoods
Jackson	—	—	—	—	0	1	—	—	—	—	—	—	—	1
Kandiyohi	—	—	—	0	1	0	0	—	—	0	0	5	0	17
Kittson	—	11	—	—	—	1	0	—	3	2	—	3	—	867
Lac Qui Parle	—	—	—	—	—	9	0	—	—	—	—	—	—	9
Lincoln	—	—	—	—	0	4	0	—	—	0	—	—	—	5
Lyon	—	—	—	—	1	5	0	—	—	0	—	—	0	8
Marshall	—	14	—	—	—	1	—	—	2	2	—	—	—	390
Martin	—	—	—	—	—	—	0	—	—	—	0	0	—	1
McLeod	—	—	—	—	—	—	0	—	—	—	1	1	0	3
Meeker	—	—	—	0	1	—	0	—	—	1	1	4	0	12
Mower	—	—	—	—	2	15	1	—	—	1	7	3	—	36
Murray	—	—	—	—	0	1	—	—	—	—	—	—	—	1
Nicollet	—	—	—	—	18	42	2	—	15	4	2	6	—	106
Nobles	—	—	—	—	0	1	—	—	—	—	—	—	—	1
Norman	—	3	—	—	—	4	1	—	0	1	—	0	—	90
Pennington	—	3	—	—	—	0	0	—	0	0	—	0	—	110
Pipestone	—	—	—	—	0	4	—	—	—	—	—	—	—	319
Polk	—	3	—	—	0	208	0	—	1	2	0	3	—	616
Pope	—	—	—	—	0	—	0	—	—	1	0	3	1	10
Red Lake	—	2	—	—	—	1	—	—	0	0	3	1	1	58
Redwood	—	—	—	—	0	16	—	—	—	—	—	—	—	17

Table 7.—Continued

	Hardwoods (continued)													
Forest Inventory Unit and county	Beech	White birch	Yellow birch	Black cherry	Black walnut	Cotton-wood	Elm	Hickory	Hard maple	Soft maple	Red oak group	White oak group	Other hardwoods	Total hardwoods
Renville	--	--	--	--	2	8	--	--	0	0	1	1	--	15
Rock	--	--	--	--	1	8	0	--	1	--	--	1	--	13
Sibley	--	--	0	--	3	2	0	0	3	1	1	2	2	14
Steele	--	--	--	0	3	19	3	--	3	0	14	5	--	64
Stevens	--	--	--	--	0	--	--	--	--	0	--	--	--	0
Swift	--	--	--	--	0	1	1	--	--	3	--	0	1	10
Waseca	--	--	--	--	13	--	0	--	2	0	1	5	0	25
Watonwan	--	--	--	--	--	--	--	--	--	--	0	--	--	1
Wilkin	--	--	--	--	--	--	--	--	--	--	--	--	--	1
Total	--	36	0	2	119	546	23	3	52	24	148	98	7	3,389
State total	14	14,362	137	59	360	1,320	143	80	2,702	6,152	6,017	1,608	42	151,792

All table cells without observations are indicated by -- . Table value of 0 indicates the volume rounds to less than 1 thousand cubic feet. Columns and rows may not add to their totals due to rounding.

48

Table 8.—Industrial roundwood production by Forest Inventory Unit, species group, and product, Minnesota, 2007

Species group	All products MCFa	Saw logs MBFb	Saw logs MCFa	Veneer logs MBFb	Veneer logs MCFa	Pulp and composite products Cordsc	Pulp and composite products MCFa	Industrial fuelwood Cordsc	Industrial fuelwood MCFa
				ALL UNITS					
Softwoods									
Eastern redcedar	31	104	21	–	–	–	–	44	3
Northern white-cedar	930	2,554	516	–	–	1,411	111	391	27
Balsam fir	13,252	5,566	1,124	–	–	154,445	12,110	248	17
Jack pine	13,135	42,893	8,664	–	–	53,584	4,201	139	10
Red pine	14,813	66,977	11,547	–	–	30,742	2,423	424	30
White pine	916	3,708	639	–	–	2,680	211	224	16
Other pine	362	5	1	–	–	4,594	360	2	0
Spruce	17,465	11,919	2,408	–	–	190,796	14,959	427	30
Tamarack	4,256	1,213	245	–	–	33,882	2,656	10,828	758
Softwood total	65,160	134,939	25,165	–	–	472,135	37,030	12,728	891
Hardwoods									
Ash	2,399	4,295	704	66	11	8,712	687	13,629	954
Aspen/balsam poplar	113,922	21,691	3,907	2,004	326	1,379,081	108,539	10,490	734
Basswood	2,473	10,068	1,649	144	23	9,269	731	466	33
Beech	14	87	14	–	–	–	–	–	–
White birch	14,362	10,679	1,749	2,332	380	145,422	11,462	8,474	593
Yellow birch	137	2	0	267	44	1,139	90	44	3
Black cherry	59	207	34	148	24	–	–	14	1
Black walnut	360	1,422	233	775	126	–	–	2	0
Cottonwood	1,320	4,725	774	–	–	6,828	538	109	8
Elm	143	765	125	51	8	–	–	107	7

Table 8.—Continued

Species group	All products MCF[a]	Saw logs MBF[b]	Saw logs MCF[a]	Veneer logs MBF[b]	Veneer logs MCF[a]	Pulp and composite products Cords[c]	Pulp and composite products MCF[a]	Industrial fuelwood Cords[c]	Industrial fuelwood MCF[a]
Hickory	80	474	78	14	2	–	–	4	0
Hard maple	2,702	3,177	520	1,112	181	24,105	1,901	1,404	98
Soft maple	6,152	1,508	247	59	10	73,039	5,756	1,966	138
Red oak group	6,017	30,307	5,601	1,622	264	263	21	1,302	91
White oak group	1,608	7,701	1,423	95	16	147	12	871	61
Other hardwoods	42	227	38	–	–	–	–	52	4
Hardwood total	151,792	97,338	17,096	8,690	1,415	1,648,005	129,735	38,934	2,725
State total	216,951	232,276	42,261	8,690	1,415	2,120,141	166,766	51,662	3,616
ASPEN-BIRCH UNIT									
Softwoods									
Northern white-cedar	860	2,280	461	–	–	1,349	106	274	19
Balsam fir	7,239	1,406	284	–	–	88,558	6,944	157	11
Jack pine	3,764	7,160	1,446	–	–	29,000	2,274	84	6
Red pine	4,772	19,698	3,396	–	–	15,515	1,223	134	9
White pine	291	1,313	226	–	–	369	29	121	8
Other pine	217	–	–	–	–	2,770	217	0	0
Spruce	11,650	6,182	1,249	–	–	131,818	10,335	325	23
Tamarack	1,983	634	128	–	–	16,722	1,311	6,255	438
Softwood total	30,777	38,673	7,190	–	–	286,100	22,438	7,348	514
Hardwoods									
Ash	1,066	559	92	5	1	5,687	448	7,498	525
Aspen/balsam poplar	38,589	7,065	1,272	1,651	269	464,636	36,569	6,170	432
Basswood	276	638	104	–	–	1,973	156	81	6

Table 8.—Continued

Species group	All products MCFa	Saw logs		Veneer logs		Pulp and composite products		Industrial fuelwood	
	MCFa	MBFb	MCFa	MBFb	MCFa	Cordsc	MCFa	Cordsc	MCFa
White birch	6,911	2,929	480	1,836	299	72,321	5,701	5,399	378
Yellow birch	65	0	0	--	--	802	63	32	2
Cottonwood	6	--	--	--	--	73	6	--	--
Elm	1	0	0	--	--	--	--	9	1
Hard maple	808	48	8	21	3	9,368	739	822	58
Soft maple	1,797	1	0	--	--	21,735	1,713	1,199	84
Red oak group	95	436	81	--	--	167	13	24	2
White oak group	21	56	10	--	--	109	9	26	2
Other hardwoods	0	0	0	--	--	--	--	1	0
Hardwood total	49,635	11,732	2,047	3,513	572	576,872	45,417	21,259	1,488
Unit total	80,411	50,405	9,237	3,513	572	862,972	67,854	28,607	2,003

CENTRAL HARDWOODS UNIT

Species group	All products MCFa	Saw logs		Veneer logs		Pulp and composite products		Industrial fuelwood	
	MCFa	MBFb	MCFa	MBFb	MCFa	Cordsc	MCFa	Cordsc	MCFa
Softwoods									
Eastern redcedar	27	84	17	--	--	--	--	44	3
Balsam fir	115	24	5	--	--	1,407	111	1	0
Jack pine	496	1,310	265	--	--	1,793	141	18	1
Red pine	808	2,139	369	--	--	3,175	250	103	7
White pine	109	545	94	--	--	131	10	43	3
Other pine	81	5	1	--	--	1,019	80	2	0
Spruce	41	21	4	--	--	457	36	11	1
Tamarack	71	29	6	--	--	244	19	656	46
Softwood total	1,751	4,156	760	--	--	8,225	647	876	61
Hardwoods									

Table 8.—Continued

Species group	All products MCF[a]	Saw logs		Veneer logs		Pulp and composite products		Industrial fuelwood	
		MBF[b]	MCF[a]	MBF[b]	MCF[a]	Cords[c]	MCF[a]	Cords[c]	MCF[a]
Ash	444	1,190	195	10	2	713	56	2,103	147
Aspen/balsam poplar	10,647	1,061	191	47	8	129,810	10,218	700	49
Basswood	577	2,749	450	39	6	1,389	109	129	9
Beech	14	87	14	–	–	–	–	–	–
White birch	745	228	37	151	25	7,394	583	151	11
Yellow birch	29	0	0	174	28	1	0	4	0
Black cherry	54	196	32	127	21	–	–	13	1
Black walnut	231	1,019	167	391	64	–	–	2	0
Cottonwood	695	1,347	221	–	–	5,923	467	102	7
Elm	118	642	105	36	6	–	–	76	5
Hickory	76	454	74	10	2	–	–	4	0
Hard maple	746	2,192	359	639	104	3,451	272	140	10
Soft maple	1,360	815	133	38	6	15,208	1,198	289	20
Red oak group	3,554	17,647	3,261	1,036	169	60	5	1,142	80
White oak group	1,256	5,973	1,104	47	8	24	2	692	48
Other hardwoods	31	165	27	–	–	–	–	32	2
Hardwood total	20,578	35,765	6,372	2,746	447	163,972	12,912	5,579	390
Unit total	22,328	39,921	7,132	2,746	447	172,197	13,558	6,455	452
NORTHERN PINE UNIT									
Softwoods									
Northern white-cedar	70	274	55	–	–	63	5	117	8
Balsam fir	5,893	4,136	835	–	–	64,416	5,050	90	6
Jack pine	8,847	34,422	6,953	–	–	22,445	1,760	38	3

Table 8.—Continued

Species group	All products MCF[a]	Saw logs MBF[b]	Saw logs MCF[a]	Veneer logs MBF[b]	Veneer logs MCF[a]	Pulp and composite products Cords[c]	Pulp and composite products MCF[a]	Industrial fuelwood Cords[c]	Industrial fuelwood MCF[a]
Red pine	9,216	45,133	7,781	—	—	11,866	935	183	13
White pine	515	1,849	319	—	—	2,179	172	56	4
Other pine	63	—	—	—	—	803	63	—	—
Spruce	5,770	5,700	1,151	—	—	58,521	4,588	92	6
Tamarack	2,194	550	111	—	—	16,824	1,319	3,917	274
Softwood total	32,568	92,064	17,206	—	—	177,116	13,891	4,494	315
Hardwoods									
Ash	792	2,041	334	51	8	2,284	180	3,849	269
Aspen/balsam poplar	62,612	13,518	2,435	305	50	758,451	59,691	3,551	249
Basswood	1,460	5,928	971	3	1	5,694	449	218	15
White birch	6,670	7,522	1,232	345	56	65,252	5,142	2,924	205
Yellow birch	43	2	0	94	15	336	26	9	1
Black cherry	3	0	0	21	3	—	—	1	0
Black walnut	9	—	—	58	9	—	—	—	—
Cottonwood	74	64	10	—	—	801	63	0	0
Elm	1	4	1	—	—	—	—	12	1
Hickory	1	—	—	4	1	—	—	—	—
Hard maple	1,095	790	129	310	50	11,226	885	442	31
Soft maple	2,971	599	98	21	3	36,026	2,839	442	31
Red oak group	2,219	11,448	2,116	560	91	36	3	136	10
White oak group	233	1,203	222	4	1	15	1	98	7
Other hardwoods	4	26	4	—	—	—	—	2	0
Hardwood total	78,190	43,145	7,553	1,775	289	880,119	69,278	11,684	818

Table 8.—Continued

Species group	All products MCF[a]	Saw logs		Veneer logs		Pulp and composite products		Industrial fuelwood	
		MBF[b]	MCF[a]	MBF[b]	MCF[a]	Cords[c]	MCF[a]	Cords[c]	MCF[a]
Unit total	110,758	135,209	24,759	1,775	289	1,057,235	83,170	16,178	1,132

PRAIRIE UNIT

Species group	All products MCF[a]	Saw logs MBF[b]	MCF[a]	Veneer logs MBF[b]	MCF[a]	Pulp Cords[c]	MCF[a]	Industrial fuelwood Cords[c]	MCF[a]
Softwoods									
Eastern redcedar	4	20	4	--	--	--	--	--	--
Balsam fir	5	--	--	--	--	66	5	--	--
Jack pine	27	1	0	--	--	346	27	--	--
Red pine	16	8	1	--	--	187	15	5	0
White pine	1	1	0	--	--	0	0	5	0
Other pine	0	--	--	--	--	2	0	--	--
Spruce	3	16	3	--	--	1	0	--	--
Tamarack	7	--	--	--	--	93	7	--	--
Softwood total	64	46	9	--	--	695	55	10	1
Hardwoods									
Ash	98	505	83	0	0	28	2	180	13
Aspen/balsam poplar	2,074	47	8	--	--	26,183	2,061	69	5
Basswood	159	753	123	101	16	213	17	38	3
White birch	36	0	0	--	--	456	36	--	--
Yellow birch	0	0	0	--	--	--	--	--	--
Black cherry	2	11	2	--	--	--	--	0	0
Black walnut	119	403	66	326	53	--	--	0	0
Cottonwood	546	3,314	543	--	--	32	3	7	1
Elm	23	120	20	15	2	--	--	10	1
Hickory	3	20	3	0	0	--	--	--	--

Table 8.—Continued

Species group	All products MCF[a]	Saw logs MBF[b]	Saw logs MCF[a]	Veneer logs MBF[b]	Veneer logs MCF[a]	Pulp and composite products Cords[c]	Pulp and composite products MCF[a]	Industrial fuelwood Cords[c]	Industrial fuelwood MCF[a]
Hard maple	52	148	24	143	23	60	5	--	--
Soft maple	24	93	15	--	--	71	6	37	3
Red oak group	148	777	144	26	4	--	--	0	0
White oak group	98	469	87	44	7	--	--	55	4
Other hardwoods	7	36	6	--	--	--	--	16	1
Hardwood total	3,389	6,695	1,124	655	107	27,043	2,128	413	29
Unit total	3,454	6,741	1,133	655	107	27,737	2,183	422	30

Species group	Cooperage MBF[b]	Cooperage MCF[a]	Poles Pieces	Poles MCF[a]	Posts M pieces[d]	Posts MCF[a]	Cabin logs MCF[a]	Excelsior/shavings MCF[a]	Misc MCF[a]
Softwoods									
Eastern redcedar	--	--	--	--	--	--	--	--	7
Northern white-cedar	--	--	29,020	160	25	20	96	--	--
Balsam fir	--	--	--	--	1	1	--	--	--
Jack pine	--	--	2,400	14	16	13	2	221	9
Red pine	--	--	31,379	188	188	150	132	335	9
White pine	--	--	2,400	14	16	13	22	--	0
Other pine	--	--	--	--	--	--	--	--	0
Spruce	--	--	--	--	1	1	67	--	0
Tamarack	--	--	--	--	--	--	20	--	577
Softwood total	--	--	65,199	377	248	198	339	556	604
Hardwoods									

Table 8.—Continued

Species group	Cooperage		Poles		Posts		Cabin logs	Excelsior/shavings	Misc
	MBF[b]	MCF[a]	Pieces	MCF[a]	M pieces[d]	MCF[a]	MCF[a]	MCF[a]	MCF[a]
Ash	--	--	--	--	--	--	0	--	44
Aspen/balsam poplar	--	--	--	--	1	1	142	250	23
Basswood	--	--	--	--	--	--	36	--	2
Beech	--	--	--	--	--	--	--	--	--
White birch	--	--	--	--	--	--	178	--	0
Yellow birch	--	--	--	--	--	--	--	--	--
Black cherry	--	--	--	--	--	--	--	--	0
Black walnut	--	--	--	--	--	--	--	--	0
Cottonwood	--	--	--	--	--	--	--	--	1
Elm	--	--	--	--	--	--	--	--	2
Hickory	--	--	--	--	--	--	--	--	0
Hard maple	--	--	--	--	--	--	--	--	1
Soft maple	--	--	--	--	--	--	--	--	2
Red oak group	--	--	--	--	--	--	1	--	39
White oak group	543	75	--	--	--	--	1	--	20
Other hardwoods	--	--	--	--	--	--	--	--	1
Hardwood total	543	75	65,199	377	1	1	358	250	137
State total	543	75	65,199	377	249	199	696	806	741

ASPEN-BIRCH UNIT

Species group	Cooperage		Poles		Posts		Cabin logs	Excelsior/shavings	Misc
	MBF[b]	MCF[a]	Pieces	MCF[a]	M pieces[d]	MCF[a]	MCF[a]	MCF[a]	MCF[a]
Softwoods									
Northern white-cedar	--	--	29,020	160	24	19	96	--	--
Balsam fir	--	--	--	--	--	--	--	--	--
Jack pine	--	--	2,400	14	16	13	--	11	--

56

Table 8.—Continued

Species group	Cooperage		Poles		Posts		Cabin logs	Excelsior/ shavings	Misc
	MBF[b]	MCF[a]	Pieces	MCF[a]	M pieces[d]	MCF[a]	MCF[a]	MCF[a]	MCF[a]
Red pine	–	–	11,640	70	46	37	21	17	–
White pine	–	–	1,440	9	10	8	11	–	–
Other pine	–	–	–	–	–	–	–	–	–
Spruce	–	–	–	–	–	–	44	–	–
Tamarack	–	–	–	–	–	–	20	–	87
Softwood total	–	–	44,500	252	96	77	191	28	87
Hardwoods									
Ash	–	–	–	–	–	–	–	–	–
Aspen/balsam poplar	–	–	–	–	–	–	43	4	–
Basswood	–	–	–	–	–	–	11	–	–
White birch	–	–	–	–	–	–	53	–	–
Yellow birch	–	–	–	–	–	–	–	–	–
Cottonwood	–	–	–	–	–	–	–	–	–
Elm	–	–	–	–	–	–	–	–	–
Hard maple	–	–	–	–	–	–	–	–	–
Soft maple	–	–	–	–	–	–	–	–	–
Red oak group	–	–	–	–	–	–	–	–	–
White oak group	–	–	–	–	–	–	–	–	–
Other hardwoods	–	–	–	–	–	–	–	–	–
Hardwood total	–	–	–	–	–	–	107	4	–
Unit total	–	–	44,500	252	96	77	298	32	87

CENTRAL HARDWOODS UNIT

Softwoods

Table 8.—Continued

Species group	Cooperage		Poles		Posts		Cabin logs	Excelsior/shavings	Misc
	MBF[b]	MCF[a]	Pieces	MCF[a]	M pieces[d]	MCF[a]	MCF[a]	MCF[a]	MCF[a]
Eastern redcedar	--	--	--	--	--	--	--	--	7
Balsam fir	--	--	--	--	--	--	--	--	--
Jack pine	--	--	--	--	--	--	0	88	1
Red pine	--	--	2,983	18	30	24	2	134	5
White pine	--	--	0	0	--	--	2	--	0
Other pine	--	--	--	--	--	--	--	--	0
Spruce	--	--	--	--	--	--	--	--	0
Tamarack	--	--	--	--	--	--	--	--	0
Softwood total	--	--	2,983	18	30	24	4	222	15
Hardwoods									
Ash	--	--	--	--	--	--	--	--	44
Aspen/balsam poplar	--	--	--	--	--	--	--	158	23
Basswood	--	--	--	--	--	--	--	--	2
Beech	--	--	--	--	--	--	--	--	--
White birch	--	--	--	--	--	--	89	--	0
Yellow birch	--	--	--	--	--	--	--	--	--
Black cherry	--	--	--	--	--	--	--	--	0
Black walnut	--	--	--	--	--	--	--	--	0
Cottonwood	--	--	--	--	--	--	--	--	1
Elm	--	--	--	--	--	--	--	--	2
Hickory	--	--	--	--	--	--	--	--	0
Hard maple	--	--	--	--	--	--	--	--	1
Soft maple	--	--	--	--	--	--	--	--	2

Table 8.—Continued

Species group	Cooperage MBF[b]	Cooperage MCF[a]	Poles Pieces	Poles MCF[a]	Posts M piecesd	Posts MCF[a]	Cabin logs MCF[a]	Excelsior/shavings MCF[a]	Misc MCF[a]
Red oak group	--	--	--	--	--	--	1	--	39
White oak group	543	75	--	--	--	--	1	--	18
Other hardwoods	--	--	--	--	--	--	--	--	1
Hardwood total	543	75	--	--	--	--	91	158	134
Unit total	543	75	2,983	18	30	24	94	380	148

NORTHERN PINE UNIT

Species group	Cooperage MBF[b]	Cooperage MCF[a]	Poles Pieces	Poles MCF[a]	Posts M piecesd	Posts MCF[a]	Cabin logs MCF[a]	Excelsior/shavings MCF[a]	Misc MCF[a]
Softwoods									
Northern white-cedar	--	--	--	--	1	1	0	--	--
Balsam fir	--	--	--	--	1	1	--	--	--
Jack pine	--	--	--	--	0	0	2	122	8
Red pine	--	--	16,756	101	112	89	109	184	4
White pine	--	--	960	6	7	5	9	--	--
Other pine	--	--	--	--	--	--	--	--	--
Spruce	--	--	--	--	1	1	24	--	--
Tamarack	--	--	--	--	--	--	--	--	490
Softwood total	--	--	17,716	106	122	98	144	306	502
Hardwoods									
Ash	--	--	--	--	--	--	0	--	--
Aspen/balsam poplar	--	--	--	--	1	1	100	88	--
Basswood	--	--	--	--	--	--	25	--	--
White birch	--	--	--	--	--	--	36	--	--
Yellow birch	--	--	--	--	--	--	--	--	--
Black cherry	--	--	--	--	--	--	--	--	--

Table 8.—Continued

Species group	Cooperage		Poles		Posts		Cabin logs	Excelsior/ shavings	Misc
	MBF[b]	MCF[a]	Pieces	MCF[a]	M piecesd	MCF[a]	MCF[a]	MCF[a]	MCF[a]
Black walnut	—	—	—	—	—	—	—	—	—
Cottonwood	—	—	—	—	—	—	—	—	—
Elm	—	—	—	—	—	—	—	—	—
Hickory	—	—	—	—	—	—	—	—	—
Hard maple	—	—	—	—	—	—	—	—	—
Soft maple	—	—	—	—	—	—	—	—	—
Red oak group	—	—	—	—	—	—	0	—	—
White oak group	—	—	—	—	—	—	—	—	2
Other hardwoods	—	—	—	—	—	—	—	—	—
Hardwood total	—	—	17,716	—	—	1	160	88	2
Unit total	—	—	—	106	124	99	304	394	504

PRAIRIE UNIT

Species group	Cooperage		Poles		Posts		Cabin logs	Excelsior/ shavings	Misc
	MBF[b]	MCF[a]	Pieces	MCF[a]	M piecesd	MCF[a]	MCF[a]	MCF[a]	MCF[a]
Softwoods									
Eastern redcedar	—	—	—	—	—	—	—	—	—
Balsam fir	—	—	—	—	—	—	—	—	—
Jack pine	—	—	—	—	—	—	—	—	0
Red pine	—	—	—	—	—	—	—	—	0
White pine	—	—	—	—	—	—	—	—	0
Other pine	—	—	—	—	—	—	—	—	—
Spruce	—	—	—	—	—	—	—	—	0
Tamarack	—	—	—	—	—	—	—	—	—
Softwood total	—	—	—	—	—	—	—	—	0
Hardwoods									

Table 8.—Continued

Species group	Cooperage		Poles		Posts		Cabin logs	Excelsior/ shavings	Misc
	MBF[b]	MCF[a]	Pieces	MCF[a]	M pieces[d]	MCF[a]	MCF[a]	MCF[a]	MCF[a]
Ash	--	--	--	--	--	--	--	--	0
Aspen/balsam poplar	--	--	--	--	--	--	--	--	0
Basswood	--	--	--	--	--	--	--	--	0
White birch	--	--	--	--	--	--	--	--	--
Yellow birch	--	--	--	--	--	--	--	--	--
Black cherry	--	--	--	--	--	--	--	--	0
Black walnut	--	--	--	--	--	--	--	--	0
Cottonwood	--	--	--	--	--	--	--	--	0
Elm	--	--	--	--	--	--	--	--	0
Hickory	--	--	--	--	--	--	--	--	0
Hard maple	--	--	--	--	--	--	--	--	0
Soft maple	--	--	--	--	--	--	--	--	0
Red oak group	--	--	--	--	--	--	--	--	0
White oak group	--	--	--	--	--	--	--	--	0
Other hardwoods	--	--	--	--	--	--	--	--	0
Hardwood total	--	--	--	--	--	--	--	--	2
Unit total	--	--	--	--	--	--	--	--	2

[a] Thousand cubic feet.

[b] Thousand board feet, International 1/4-inch rule.

[c] Standard cords are 128 cubic feet consisting of 85 cubic feet of wood and 43 cubic feet of bark and air space.

[d] Thousand pieces.

All table cells without observations are indicated by --. Table value of 0 indicates the volume less than 1/2 unit of measure. Columns and rows may not add to their totals due to rounding.

Table 9.—Saw log receipts and production, in thousand board feet, International 1/4-inch rule, by Forest Inventory Unit and species group, Minnesota, 2004 and 2007

Species group	Receipts			Production		
	2004	2007	Percent change	2004	2007	Percent change
Softwood						
Eastern redcedar	49	104	112%	48	104	117%
Northern white-cedar	3,212	2,554	-20%	3,202	2,554	-20%
Cypress	—	8	—	—	—	—
Balsam fir	5,058	5,546	10%	4,198	5,566	33%
Jack pine	74,120	48,825	-34%	69,564	42,893	-38%
Red pine	62,725	74,215	18%	54,690	66,977	22%
White pine	4,932	4,417	-10%	4,290	3,708	-14%
Other pine	—	5	—	—	5	—
Spruce	12,062	13,274	10%	9,505	11,919	25%
Tamarack	827	1,213	47%	825	1,213	47%
Softwood total	162,984	150,159	-8%	146,322	134,939	-8%
Hardwood						
Ash	3,958	4,120	4%	4,100	4,295	5%
Aspen/balsam poplar	37,618	24,354	-35%	34,417	21,691	-37%
Basswood	10,921	9,780	-10%	11,235	10,068	-10%
Beech			87	87		0%
White birch	11,399	10,771	-6%	11,330	10,679	-6%
Yellow birch	5	2	-60%	5	2	-60%
Other birch	0	—	—	0	—	—
Black cherry	205	73	-64%	254	207	-19%
Black walnut	778	1,392	79%	878	1,422	62%
Cottonwood	4,616	5,015	9%	5,705	4,725	-17%

Table 9.—Continued

Species group	Receipts			Production		
	2004	2007	Percent change	2004	2007	Percent change
Elm	813	658	-19%	892	765	-14%
Hickory	273	215	-21%	414	474	14%
Hard maple	4,164	2,484	-40%	4,664	3,177	-32%
Soft maple	964	1,229	27%	1,171	1,508	29%
Red oak group	25,253	23,173	-8%	29,752	30,307	2%
White oak group	4,666	5,909	27%	5,681	7,701	36%
Other hardwoods	132	223	69%	191	228	19%
Hardwood total	105,766	89,398	-15%	110,777	97,338	-12%
All species	268,750	239,557	-11%	257,099	232,276	-10%

All table cells without observations are indicated by — . Table value of 0 indicates the volume rounds to less than 1 thousand board feet. Columns and rows may not add to their totals due to rounding.

Table 10.—Wood material harvested for industrial roundwood, in thousand cubic feet, by Forest Inventory Unit, source of material, and species group, Minnesota, 2007[a]

Species group	Source of material						
	Growing stock				Non-growing stock		
	Used for products		Logging residue (not used)	Total growing stock	Used for products		Cull trees
	Sawtimber	Pole-timber			Limbwood	Saplings	
	ALL UNITS						
Softwoods							
Eastern redcedar	23.3	6.0	2.9	32.1	1.2	0.0	0.5
Northern white-cedar	665.1	207.1	59.9	932.1	20.1	0.7	26.4
Balsam fir	8,555.5	4,178.7	338.9	13,073.1	481.4	0.1	14.1
Jack pine	10,413.5	2,218.6	852.1	13,484.2	266.2	0.4	97.2
Red pine	13,520.3	833.7	457.2	14,811.2	205.7	5.0	175.8
White pine	812.6	65.7	25.0	903.3	16.5	0.5	14.8
Other pines	225.8	123.0	7.5	356.3	12.9	0.0	0.0
Tamarack	2,380.6	1,454.0	165.4	4,000.0	336.4	2.2	78.7
Spruce	11,520.7	5,297.9	513.4	17,332.0	576.3	0.1	30.1
Softwood total	48,117.4	14,384.6	2,422.4	64,924.4	1,916.7	9.0	437.6
Hardwoods							
Ash	1,116.9	797.2	195.3	2,109.4	330.4	6.3	147.1
Aspen/balsam poplar	78,344.6	30,411.2	6,050.9	114,806.7	1,416.9	21.8	3,711.5
Basswood	1,785.0	552.0	411.4	2,748.4	44.6	2.1	89.1
Beech	12.6	1.2	3.3	17.1	0.1	--	0.4
White birch	6,362.6	6,695.0	875.7	13,933.3	595.2	41.9	653.9
Yellow birch	74.6	49.9	10.6	135.1	3.4	0.0	8.7
Black cherry	52.2	3.3	11.9	67.3	0.6	0.0	3.5
Black walnut	319.3	19.2	74.3	412.8	1.7	0.0	19.5

Table 10.—Continued

	Source of material						
	Growing stock				Non-growing stock		
	Used for products		Logging residue (not used)	Total growing stock	Used for products		
Species group	Sawtimber	Pole-timber			Limbwood	Saplings	Cull trees
Cottonwood	891.4	358.6	195.1	1,445.1	21.5	0.0	49.0
Elm	120.9	13.5	30.4	164.8	3.1	0.0	5.4
Hickory	70.8	6.5	18.1	95.3	0.6	0.0	2.6
Hard maple	1,212.1	1,184.5	191.5	2,588.1	153.8	30.7	111.4
Soft maple	2,434.9	3,213.5	257.2	5,905.6	213.6	7.2	281.0
Red oak group	4,078.8	83.1	1,268.3	5,430.2	130.4	0.6	1,699.8
White oak group	1,073.3	41.2	326.4	1,440.9	49.4	0.3	437.1
Other hardwoods	34.4	4.7	8.8	47.9	1.4	0.0	1.5
Hardwood total	97,984.6	43,434.4	9,929.0	151,348.0	2,966.9	110.8	7,221.4
State total	146,102.0	57,819.0	12,351.4	216,272.4	4,883.6	119.8	7,659.0

ASPEN-BIRCH UNIT

Softwoods							
Northern white-cedar	610.8	197.4	55.1	863.4	16.7	0.7	24.9
Balsam fir	4,588.3	2,364.3	163.7	7,116.3	274.4	0.0	4.2
Jack pine	2,717.8	899.9	171.7	3,789.4	104.0	0.4	18.2
Red pine	4,268.5	323.2	132.1	4,723.8	75.6	1.2	68.4
White pine	264.5	15.4	8.6	288.5	5.9	0.3	4.4
Other pines	135.5	74.0	4.4	213.9	7.8	0.0	0.0
Spruce	7,591.5	3,626.7	319.5	11,537.8	394.3	0.1	16.3
Tamarack	1,092.9	655.0	52.5	1,800.5	186.3	1.3	45.4
Softwood total	21,269.9	8,155.9	907.6	30,333.4	1,064.8	4.0	181.7

Table 10.—Continued

| Species group | Growing stock | | | | Non-growing stock | | |
| | Used for products | | Logging residue (not used) | Total growing stock | Used for products | | Cull trees |
	Sawtimber	Pole-timber			Limbwood	Saplings	
Hardwoods							
Ash	357.3	446.8	35.0	839.2	182.5	3.7	74.5
Aspen/balsam poplar	26,432.4	10,304.3	2,029.7	38,766.5	553.1	9.8	1,282.1
Basswood	154.8	99.4	30.5	284.8	9.9	1.5	10.3
White birch	2,857.7	3,347.2	349.9	6,554.8	340.4	30.2	325.6
Yellow birch	24.8	35.1	2.2	62.2	2.4	0.0	3.1
Cottonwood	2.2	3.1	0.2	5.5	0.2	—	0.3
Elm	0.1	0.2	0.0	0.4	0.2	0.0	0.1
Hard maple	194.6	473.5	11.4	679.4	85.1	21.1	27.1
Soft maple	651.0	972.7	56.9	1,680.6	83.1	5.1	83.6
Red oak group	59.9	8.1	17.9	85.9	2.3	0.0	24.7
White oak group	10.8	5.4	2.6	18.7	1.0	0.0	3.7
Other hardwoods	0.1	0.0	0.0	0.1	0.0	0.0	0.0
Hardwood total	30,745.6	15,696.0	2,536.3	48,977.9	1,260.2	71.4	1,835.1
Unit total	52,015.5	23,851.9	3,443.9	79,311.3	2,325.0	75.4	2,016.8

CENTRAL HARDWOODS UNIT

Species group	Sawtimber	Pole-timber	Logging residue (not used)	Total growing stock	Limbwood	Saplings	Cull trees
Softwoods							
Eastern redcedar	19.7	5.7	2.5	27.9	1.2	0.0	0.5
Balsam fir	75.5	24.2	1.7	101.3	14.1	0.0	0.1
Jack pine	372.5	104.7	38.7	515.9	11.5	0.0	3.0

Table 10.—Continued

Species group	Source of material						
	Growing stock					Non-growing stock	
	Used for products		Logging residue (not used)	Total growing stock	Limbwood	Used for products	
	Sawtimber	Pole-timber				Saplings	Cull trees
Red pine	633.6	132.6	38.8	804.9	19.8	0.8	13.7
White pine	102.0	3.7	3.0	108.7	2.2	0.0	1.2
Other pines	51.0	27.5	1.8	80.3	2.9	0.0	0.0
Spruce	26.4	12.9	1.1	40.5	1.6	0.0	0.1
Tamarack	27.3	23.7	0.9	51.9	15.2	0.1	4.7
Softwood total	1,307.9	335.1	88.5	1,731.5	68.4	0.9	23.3
Hardwoods							
Ash	252.9	114.7	57.7	425.3	51.6	1.6	22.7
Aspen/balsam poplar	7,164.1	2,943.9	568.5	10,676.6	186.2	8.5	337.4
Basswood	446.3	101.0	107.5	654.9	9.3	0.4	20.0
Beech	12.6	1.2	3.3	17.1	0.1	—	0.4
White birch	303.5	356.4	44.9	704.8	43.5	10.6	27.4
Yellow birch	25.6	0.1	4.8	30.5	0.1	0.0	2.8
Black cherry	47.4	3.1	10.9	61.3	0.5	0.0	3.1
Black walnut	204.6	13.8	48.7	267.0	1.2	0.0	11.3
Cottonwood	376.1	274.3	66.9	717.4	16.0	0.0	28.8
Elm	100.2	11.0	25.3	136.5	2.3	0.0	4.3
Hickory	67.3	6.2	17.2	90.7	0.5	0.0	2.5
Hard maple	469.8	202.7	101.6	774.1	32.9	8.9	29.0
Soft maple	580.6	674.0	73.1	1,327.7	43.1	1.8	60.4
Red oak group	2,403.4	58.6	745.3	3,207.3	84.2	0.4	993.6

Table 10.—Continued

	Source of material						
	Growing stock		Logging residue (not used)	Total growing stock	Non-growing stock		Cull trees
	Used for products				Used for products		
Species group	Sawtimber	Pole-timber			Limbwood	Saplings	
White oak group	842.7	29.1	255.0	1,126.8	39.4	0.2	339.8
Other hardwoods	25.1	3.4	6.4	34.9	0.9	0.0	1.0
Hardwood total	13,322.3	4,793.4	2,137.1	20,252.8	512.0	32.5	1,884.5
Unit total	14,630.2	5,128.5	2,225.6	21,984.3	580.4	33.4	1,907.7
NORTHERN PINE UNIT							
Softwoods							
Northern white-cedar	54.3	9.6	4.8	68.7	3.5	0.1	1.5
Balsam fir	3,888.5	1,788.5	173.4	5,850.4	192.7	0.0	9.8
Jack pine	7,306.1	1,204.7	641.2	9,152.0	149.8	0.0	76.0
Red pine	8,606.9	374.2	286.0	9,267.1	110.0	2.9	93.1
White pine	445.8	46.4	13.5	505.6	8.3	0.2	9.2
Other pines	39.3	21.4	1.3	62.0	2.2	—	—
Spruce	3,899.7	1,657.9	192.5	5,750.2	180.4	0.0	13.6
Tamarack	1,255.9	772.8	111.8	2,140.4	134.7	0.8	28.6
Softwood total	25,496.4	5,875.6	1,424.5	32,796.4	781.5	4.1	231.9
Hardwoods							
Ash	430.1	223.1	83.6	736.9	91.8	0.9	46.1
Aspen/balsam poplar	43,311.3	16,614.3	3,344.5	63,270.1	657.8	3.5	2,023.3
Basswood	1,053.1	331.3	242.0	1,626.4	23.4	0.3	52.3
White birch	3,187.6	2,971.9	479.6	6,639.2	210.3	1.1	299.2

Table 10.—Continued

	Source of material						
	Growing stock				Non-growing stock		
	Used for products		Logging residue	Total	Used for products		
Species group	Sawtimber	Pole-timber	(not used)	growing stock	Limbwood	Saplings	Cull trees
Yellow birch	24.3	14.6	3.6	42.5	0.9	0.0	2.8
Black cherry	3.1	0.0	0.6	3.7	0.0	0.0	0.3
Black walnut	8.5	—	1.6	10.1	0.0	—	0.9
Cottonwood	33.5	35.1	4.6	73.2	1.8	0.0	3.2
Elm	0.7	0.3	0.1	1.2	0.3	0.0	0.1
Hickory	0.6	—	0.1	0.7	0.0	—	0.1
Soft maple	1,187.1	1,561.5	123.6	2,872.2	86.3	0.2	136.0
Hard maple	503.4	503.7	68.8	1,075.9	35.5	0.7	52.0
Red oak group	1,514.6	15.6	473.3	2,003.6	41.3	0.2	638.5
White oak group	154.0	4.9	48.8	207.7	6.3	0.1	66.8
Other hardwoods	3.7	0.4	1.0	5.1	0.1	0.0	0.1
Hardwood total	51,415.6	22,276.8	4,875.9	78,568.4	1,155.7	6.8	3,321.9
Unit total	76,912.0	28,152.4	6,300.4	111,364.8	1,937.2	10.9	3,553.8
PRAIRIE UNIT							
Softwoods:							
Eastern redcedar	3.6	0.3	0.3	4.2	0.1	—	0.0
Balsam fir	3.2	1.7	0.1	5.1	0.2	—	—
Jack pine	17.1	9.3	0.6	27.0	1.0	—	0.0
Red pine	11.3	3.7	0.3	15.3	0.4	0.0	0.6
White pine	0.3	0.2	0.0	0.5	0.1	0.0	0.0
Other pines	0.1	0.1	0.0	0.1	0.0	—	—

Table 10.—Continued

	Source of material						
	Growing stock				Non-growing stock		
	Used for products		Logging residue (not used)	Total growing stock	Used for products		Cull trees
Species group	Sawtimber	Pole-timber			Limbwood	Saplings	
Spruce	3.0	0.3	0.3	3.6	0.0	--	0.0
Tamarack	4.6	2.5	0.1	7.2	0.3	--	--
Softwood total	43.2	18.0	1.8	63.0	2.0	0.0	0.7
Hardwoods							
Ash	76.6	12.5	18.9	108.0	4.5	0.0	3.9
Aspen/balsam poplar	1,436.8	548.7	108.1	2,093.5	19.9	0.0	68.6
Basswood	130.7	20.2	31.4	182.3	2.1	0.0	6.4
White birch	13.8	19.5	1.3	34.6	1.0	--	1.6
Yellow birch	0.0	0.0	0.0	0.0	0.0	--	0.0
Black cherry	1.7	0.2	0.4	2.3	0.0	0.0	0.1
Black walnut	106.2	5.5	24.0	135.6	0.5	0.0	7.2
Cottonwood	479.7	46.0	123.4	649.0	3.5	0.0	16.7
Elm	19.9	1.9	4.9	26.8	0.3	0.0	0.9
Hickory	2.9	0.3	0.7	3.9	0.0	--	0.1
Hard maple	44.3	4.6	9.7	58.6	0.3	--	3.2
Soft maple	16.2	5.3	3.7	25.2	1.1	0.0	1.0
Red oak group	100.9	0.7	31.8	133.5	2.6	0.0	43.1
White oak group	65.9	1.8	20.0	87.7	2.8	0.0	26.8
Other hardwoods	5.5	0.9	1.4	7.8	0.4	0.0	0.3
Hardwood total	2,501.1	668.1	379.7	3,548.9	39.0	0.1	179.9
Unit total	2,544.3	686.2	381.5	3,612.0	41.0	0.1	180.6

Table 10.—Continued

| Species group | Non-growing stock | | | | | |
| | Used for Products | | | | | |
	Dead trees	Logging slash (not used)	Total non-growing stock	Total used	Total not used	Total harvested
			ALL UNITS			
Softwood						
Eastern redcedar	0.3	12.5	14.6	31.4	15.4	46.8
Northern white-cedar	10.3	428.8	486.4	929.8	488.8	1,418.5
Balsam fir	22.5	6,437.3	6,955.3	13,252.2	6,776.2	20,028.3
Jack pine	138.6	6,984.8	7,487.4	13,134.6	7,837.0	20,971.6
Red pine	72.7	5,550.5	6,009.6	14,813.2	6,007.6	20,820.8
White pine	6.3	346.0	384.1	916.3	371.0	1,287.4
Other pines	0.0	174.8	187.7	361.8	182.3	544.0
Tamarack	4.2	1,506.3	1,927.7	4,256.0	1,671.7	5,927.7
Spruce	39.5	8,642.5	9,288.5	17,464.6	9,156.0	26,620.6
Softwood total	294.5	30,083.5	32,741.4	65,159.8	32,505.9	97,665.8
Hardwoods						
Ash	1.1	753.5	1,238.5	2,399.1	948.8	3,347.9
Aspen/balsam poplar	16.1	46,896.4	52,062.7	113,922.1	52,947.3	166,869.4
Basswood	0.7	1,282.6	1,419.2	2,473.4	1,694.1	4,167.5
Beech	—	7.8	8.4	14.3	11.1	25.4
White birch	13.0	6,659.3	7,963.3	14,361.6	7,534.9	21,896.6
Yellow birch	—	59.5	71.6	136.6	70.0	206.7
Black cherry	—	25.9	30.0	59.4	37.8	97.3
Black walnut	—	165.7	186.8	359.7	239.9	599.6

Table 10.—Continued

| Species group | Non-growing stock | | Total non-growing stock | Total used | Total not used | Total harvested |
| | Used for Products | Logging slash | | | | |
	Dead trees	(not used)				
Cottonwood	--	698.4	768.9	1,320.5	893.6	2,214.0
Elm	--	71.5	80.0	142.9	101.8	244.8
Hickory	--	43.2	46.3	80.4	61.2	141.7
Hard maple	9.8	1,013.7	1,319.5	2,702.3	1,205.2	3,907.5
Soft maple	2.2	3,020.6	3,524.6	6,152.4	3,277.8	9,430.2
Red oak group	24.4	3,913.5	5,768.7	6,017.1	5,181.9	11,198.9
White oak group	6.2	1,001.7	1,494.7	1,607.5	1,328.0	2,935.6
Other hardwoods	0.0	20.7	23.5	42.1	29.4	71.6
Hardwood total	73.5	65,634.0	76,006.5	151,791.5	75,563.0	227,354.5
State total	368.0	95,717.5	108,747.9	216,951.3	108,068.9	325,020.3
ASPEN-BIRCH UNIT						
Softwoods						
Northern white-cedar	9.4	394.1	445.8	859.9	449.2	1,309.1
Balsam fir	7.5	3,480.1	3,766.2	7,238.7	3,643.8	10,882.5
Jack pine	23.8	1,921.5	2,068.0	3,764.1	2,093.2	5,857.3
Red pine	35.5	1,820.2	2,000.9	4,772.5	1,952.3	6,724.7
White pine	1.1	105.8	117.4	291.4	114.4	405.8
Other pines	--	105.0	112.8	217.2	109.4	326.6
Spruce	20.8	5,731.3	6,162.8	11,649.7	6,050.8	17,700.5
Tamarack	2.3	745.1	980.3	1,983.2	797.6	2,780.8
Softwood total	100.4	14,303.1	15,654.0	30,776.7	15,210.7	45,987.4

Table 10.—Continued

Species group	Non-growing stock			Total used	Total not used	Total harvested
	Used for Products — Dead trees	Logging slash (not used)	Total non-growing stock			
Hardwoods						
Ash	0.7	283.5	545.0	1,065.6	318.6	1,384.2
Aspen/balsam poplar	7.0	15,774.9	17,626.8	38,588.7	17,804.6	56,393.3
Basswood	0.5	128.4	150.5	276.4	158.9	435.3
White birch	9.4	3,026.0	3,731.7	6,910.6	3,375.9	10,286.5
Yellow birch	--	32.4	37.9	65.4	34.7	100.1
Cottonwood	--	2.9	3.3	5.7	3.1	8.8
Elm	--	0.0	0.3	0.6	0.0	0.6
Hard maple	6.8	177.9	318.0	808.2	189.3	997.5
Soft maple	1.6	831.5	1,005.0	1,797.1	888.4	2,685.5
Red oak group	0.3	61.7	89.1	95.4	79.6	175.0
White oak group	0.0	11.6	16.3	20.8	14.2	35.0
Other hardwoods	--	0.0	0.1	0.1	0.0	0.2
Hardwood total	26.3	20,330.9	23,524.0	49,634.6	22,867.3	72,501.9
Unit total	126.8	34,634.0	39,178.0	80,411.3	38,078.0	118,489.3

CENTRAL HARDWOODS UNIT

Species group	Used for Products — Dead trees	Logging slash (not used)	Total non-growing stock	Total used	Total not used	Total harvested
Softwoods						
Eastern redcedar	0.3	10.2	12.2	27.3	12.8	40.1
Balsam fir	1.7	35.7	51.6	115.5	37.4	152.9
Jack pine	4.6	218.7	237.9	496.4	257.4	753.8
Red pine	7.9	243.6	285.8	808.3	282.4	1,090.8
White pine	0.3	41.7	45.4	109.5	44.7	154.2

73

Table 10.—Continued

Species group	Non-growing stock		Total non-growing stock	Total used	Total not used	Total harvested
	Used for Products					
	Dead trees	Logging slash (not used)				
Other pines	0.0	39.3	42.2	81.5	41.0	122.5
Spruce	0.1	19.8	21.5	41.1	20.9	62.0
Tamarack	0.1	14.9	34.9	71.1	15.8	86.8
Softwood total	14.9	623.9	731.5	1,750.6	712.4	2,463.0
Hardwoods						
Ash	0.4	133.4	209.7	443.9	191.2	635.0
Aspen/balsam poplar	6.8	4,133.8	4,672.7	10,647.0	4,702.3	15,349.3
Basswood	0.1	300.9	330.8	577.3	408.4	985.6
Beech	–	7.8	8.4	14.3	11.1	25.4
White birch	3.4	270.2	355.1	744.8	315.1	1,059.9
Yellow birch	–	8.7	11.6	28.6	13.4	42.0
Black cherry	–	23.9	27.5	54.0	34.7	88.8
Black walnut	–	110.6	123.1	230.9	159.2	390.1
Cottonwood	–	359.6	404.4	695.3	426.5	1,121.8
Elm	–	59.6	66.2	117.9	84.8	202.7
Hickory	–	41.2	44.2	76.5	58.4	134.9
Hard maple	2.9	278.7	352.5	746.2	380.4	1,126.6
Soft maple	0.6	671.4	777.2	1,360.4	744.5	2,104.9
Red oak group	14.2	2,281.5	3,374.0	3,554.4	3,026.9	6,581.3
White oak group	4.8	776.3	1,160.5	1,256.0	1,031.3	2,287.3
Other hardwoods	–	15.1	16.9	30.5	21.4	52.0

Table 10.—Continued

	Non-growing stock					
	Used for Products					
Species group	Dead trees	Logging slash (not used)	Total non-growing stock	Total used	Total not used	Total harvested
Hardwood total	33.2	9,472.6	11,934.7	20,577.9	11,609.7	32,187.5
Unit total	48.1	10,096.5	12,666.2	22,328.4	12,322.1	34,650.5

NORTHERN PINE UNIT

Species group	Dead trees	Logging slash (not used)	Total non-growing stock	Total used	Total not used	Total harvested
Softwoods						
Northern white-cedar	0.9	34.7	40.7	69.9	39.5	109.4
Balsam fir	13.3	2,919.0	3,134.8	5,892.9	3,092.4	8,985.2
Jack pine	110.2	4,831.4	5,167.3	8,846.8	5,472.5	14,319.3
Red pine	28.9	3,480.2	3,715.1	9,216.0	3,766.2	12,982.2
White pine	5.0	198.4	221.0	514.9	211.8	726.7
Other pines	—	30.4	32.7	63.0	31.7	94.7
Spruce	18.6	2,889.5	3,102.2	5,770.3	3,082.0	8,852.3
Tamarack	1.8	742.9	908.7	2,194.5	854.7	3,049.2
Softwood total	178.6	15,126.4	16,322.5	32,568.1	16,550.8	49,118.9
Hardwoods						
Ash	0.0	289.6	428.4	792.1	373.2	1,165.3
Aspen/balsam poplar	2.3	26,124.4	28,811.2	62,612.4	29,468.9	92,081.3
Basswood	0.1	772.2	848.3	1,460.4	1,014.3	2,474.7
White birch	0.2	3,344.7	3,855.5	6,670.3	3,824.3	10,494.6
Yellow birch	—	18.3	22.0	42.6	21.9	64.5
Black cherry	—	1.0	1.4	3.4	1.6	5.1
Black walnut	—	2.9	3.8	9.5	4.5	14.0

Table 10.—Continued

| Species group | Non-growing stock | | | | | |
	Used for Products Dead trees	Logging slash (not used)	Total non-growing stock	Total used	Total not used	Total harvested
Cottonwood	--	38.0	42.9	73.6	42.6	116.2
Elm	--	0.4	0.7	1.4	0.5	1.9
Hickory	--	0.2	0.3	0.7	0.3	1.0
Soft maple	0.1	1,506.4	1,729.1	2,971.2	1,630.0	4,601.2
Hard maple	0.2	534.4	622.7	1,095.4	603.2	1,698.6
Red oak group	9.2	1,471.1	2,160.2	2,219.4	1,944.4	4,163.8
White oak group	1.0	152.4	226.5	233.0	201.1	434.2
Other hardwoods	--	2.3	2.5	4.4	3.2	7.6
Hardwood total	12.9	34,258.2	38,755.6	78,189.8	39,134.2	117,324.0
Unit total	191.6	49,384.6	55,078.1	110,757.9	55,685.0	166,442.9
			PRAIRIE UNIT			
Softwoods						
Eastern redcedar	0.1	2.3	2.5	4.0	2.6	6.7
Balsam fir	--	2.5	2.7	5.1	2.6	7.7
Jack pine	0.0	13.2	14.2	27.4	13.8	41.2
Red pine	0.4	6.5	7.9	16.4	6.8	23.2
White pine	0.0	0.1	0.2	0.6	0.1	0.7
Other pines	--	0.1	0.1	0.1	0.1	0.2
Spruce	0.1	1.9	2.1	3.5	2.2	5.7
Tamarack	--	3.5	3.8	7.3	3.7	11.0
Softwood total	0.5	30.1	33.4	64.5	31.9	96.4

Table 10.—Continued

Species group	Used for Products Dead trees	Non-growing stock Logging slash (not used)	Total non-growing stock	Total used	Total not used	Total harvested
Hardwoods						
Ash	—	46.9	55.4	97.5	65.8	163.4
Aspen/balsam poplar	—	863.3	951.9	2,074.0	971.4	3,045.4
Basswood	—	81.1	89.6	159.4	112.6	272.0
White birch	—	18.4	21.0	35.9	19.6	55.6
Yellow birch	—	0.0	0.0	0.0	0.0	0.1
Black cherry	—	1.0	1.1	2.0	1.5	3.4
Black walnut	—	52.2	59.9	119.3	76.2	195.5
Cottonwood	—	297.9	318.2	545.9	421.3	967.2
Elm	—	11.5	12.8	23.1	16.5	39.5
Hickory	—	1.8	1.9	3.3	2.5	5.8
Hard maple	—	22.7	26.3	52.5	32.4	84.9
Soft maple	—	11.3	13.3	23.5	15.0	38.5
Red oak group	0.6	99.2	145.4	147.9	131.0	278.9
White oak group	0.4	61.4	91.4	97.7	81.4	179.1
Other hardwoods	—	3.3	4.0	7.2	4.7	11.8
Hardwood total	1.0	1,572.2	1,792.2	3,389.2	1,951.9	5,341.1
Unit total	1.5	1,602.3	1,825.6	3,453.7	1,983.8	5,437.5

[a] Based on factors obtained from regional utilization studies.

All table cells without observations are indicated by —. Table value of 0.0 indicates the volume rounds to less than 0.1 thousand cubic feet. Columns and rows may not add to their totals due to rounding.

Table 11.—Growing-stock removals from timberland for industrial roundwood, in thousand cubic feet, by Forest Inventory Unit, county, and species group, Minnesota, 2007

Forest Inventory Unit and county	All species	Softwoods										Hardwoods		
		Northern											Aspen/	
		Eastern redcedar	White-cedar	Balsam fir	Jack pine	Red pine	White pine	Other pine	Spruce	Tama-rack	Total softwoods	Ash	balsam poplar	Bass-wood
Aspen-Birch Unit														
Carlton	5,005	—	5	348	36	684	8	33	157	31	1,302	183	2,814	28
Cook	2,664	—	3	137	63	462	45	83	655	0	1,448	0	1,036	—
Koochiching	18,694	—	690	1,738	535	600	47	1	3,966	849	8,427	99	9,210	121
Lake	6,856	—	6	814	352	517	28	16	977	56	2,764	77	2,416	47
St. Louis	46,093	—	160	4,080	2,803	2,461	160	82	5,783	863	16,392	479	23,291	89
Total	79,311	—	863	7,116	3,789	4,724	288	214	11,538	1,800	30,333	839	38,766	285
Central Hardwoods Unit														
Anoka	93	0	—	—	1	37	6	—	—	0	43	7	14	0
Benton	79	0	—	—	13	22	—	0	0	1	36	0	19	3
Carver	60	1	—	—	—	—	—	—	—	—	1	1	—	—
Chisago	287	0	—	—	0	28	7	0	0	0	36	14	62	8
Dakota	43	—	—	—	2	2	2	—	—	—	6	5	2	0
Douglas	599	—	—	0	252	0	0	—	0	0	253	9	10	25
Fillmore	766	1	—	—	—	1	1	0	1	—	4	32	3	63
Goodhue	508	1	—	—	—	0	0	—	1	—	3	26	42	94
Hennepin	108	6	—	—	—	1	1	—	—	—	7	21	10	3
Houston	1,349	—	—	—	—	0	—	—	—	—	0	20	20	62
Isanti	311	0	—	—	13	13	28	0	0	1	56	18	78	5
Kanabec	1,645	0	—	0	1	18	11	—	0	11	41	20	1,213	62
Le Sueur	65	0	—	—	0	0	0	—	0	—	1	4	—	2
Mille Lacs	1,538	—	—	—	14	10	7	—	0	6	37	20	1,010	50

Table 11.—Continued

Forest Inventory Unit and county	All species	Softwoods										Hardwoods		
		Eastern redcedar	Northern white-cedar	Balsam fir	Jack pine	Red pine	White pine	Other pine	Spruce	Tama-rack	Total softwoods	Ash	Aspen/ balsam poplar	Bass-wood
Morrison	2,006	0	—	—	31	46	5	1	1	4	88	9	1,806	6
Olmsted	261	—	—	—	0	1	0	—	0	—	1	10	1	19
Otter Tail	797	—	—	0	16	14	11	0	0	5	47	13	588	25
Pine	8,387	1	—	98	120	485	5	78	35	19	840	79	5,320	49
Ramsey	46	—	—	—	1	2	1	0	0	—	5	13	8	—
Rice	92	1	—	—	—	—	—	—	—	—	1	4	0	5
Scott	129	2	—	—	—	—	—	—	—	—	2	11	2	2
Sherburne	90	0	—	0	13	27	0	0	0	0	40	14	11	0
Steams	161	0	—	—	—	30	1	—	0	0	32	10	21	10
Todd	1,020	9	—	3	38	32	4	0	—	5	91	13	393	66
Wabasha	648	2	—	—	—	12	6	—	1	—	20	10	10	54
Washington	47	0	—	—	—	2	1	—	—	0	3	10	4	0
Winona	731	—	—	—	—	3	10	—	0	—	13	17	26	33
Wright	118	2	—	—	—	20	1	—	—	—	24	14	4	8
Total	21,984	28	—	101	516	805	109	80	40	52	1,732	425	10,677	655
Northern Pine Unit														
Aitkin	13,810	—	2	393	212	399	48	8	459	207	1,727	289	7,714	619
Becker	4,664	—	—	326	323	342	26	8	42	18	1,085	13	2,998	60
Beltrami	17,331	—	28	1,286	830	579	75	1	1,044	463	4,307	56	11,673	105
Cass	14,658	—	2	244	1,831	2,552	183	2	190	174	5,179	84	6,961	288
Clearwater	5,009	—	—	240	49	179	59	0	300	86	913	8	3,533	127

Table 11.—Continued

Forest Inventory Unit and county	All species	Softwoods											Hardwoods		
		Northern									Total softwoods		Ash	Aspen/ balsam poplar	Basswood
		Eastern redcedar	Northern white-cedar	Balsam fir	Jack pine	Red pine	White pine	Other pine	Spruce	Tamarack					
Crow Wing	5,024	–	14	36	517	713	25	20	27	15	1,368		29	3,138	50
Hubbard	10,818	–	–	354	1,260	1,631	27	11	161	107	3,550		15	6,345	53
Itasca	28,940	–	21	2,575	1,886	1,828	52	10	2,807	583	9,763		213	15,301	238
Lake of the Woods	5,014	–	2	287	840	217	0	0	505	438	2,289		11	2,499	10
Mahnomen	832	–	–	5	10	24	0	0	0	2	41		6	686	39
Roseau	1,510	–	–	95	301	95	0	0	212	28	731		3	693	12
Wadena	3,756	–	–	10	1,094	709	10	0	3	19	1,845		9	1,729	27
Total	111,365	–	69	5,850	9,152	9,267	506	62	5,750	2,140	32,796		737	63,270	1,626
Prairie Unit															
Big Stone	21	0	–	–	–	–	–	–	–	–	0		0	–	–
Blue Earth	148	1	–	–	–	1	0	–	–	–	2		3	0	1
Brown	112	0	–	–	–	0	–	–	–	–	0		2	–	1
Chippewa	9	0	–	–	–	0	–	–	–	–	0		3	–	–
Clay	50	–	–	–	–	–	–	–	–	–	–		5	0	36
Cottonwood	5	–	–	–	–	0	0	–	0	–	1		1	–	–
Dodge	20	–	–	–	0	0	0	–	0	–	0		0	1	1
Faribault	186	–	–	–	–	–	–	–	1	–	1		10	–	19
Freeborn	76	–	–	–	–	–	–	–	–	–	–		15	–	–
Grant	1	–	–	–	–	–	–	–	–	–	–		–	–	0
Jackson	2	–	–	–	–	–	–	–	0	–	0		0	–	–
Kandiyohi	16	1	–	–	–	–	–	–	–	–	1		6	0	2

Table 11.—Continued

Forest Inventory Unit and county	All species	Softwoods										Hardwoods		
		Eastern redcedar	Northern white-cedar	Balsam fir	Jack pine	Red pine	White pine	Other pine	Spruce	Tama-rack	Total softwoods	Ash	Aspen/ balsam poplar	Bass-wood
Kittson	887	—	—	0	8	4	—	0	0	2	15	1	850	3
Lac Qui Parle	11	0	—	—	—	—	—	—	—	—	0	0	—	—
Lincoln	7	—	—	—	—	0	—	—	—	—	0	1	—	—
Lyon	10	—	—	—	—	0	—	—	0	—	0	2	0	—
Marshall	412	—	—	0	10	5	0	—	0	3	18	1	372	3
Martin	1	—	—	—	—	—	—	—	—	—	—	0	—	—
McLeod	3	—	—	—	—	—	—	—	—	—	—	0	0	0
Meeker	13	1	—	—	—	—	—	—	—	—	1	4	0	1
Mower	40	—	—	—	—	—	—	—	—	—	—	8	—	0
Murray	2	—	—	—	—	—	—	—	0	—	0	0	0	—
Nicollet	119	1	—	—	—	—	—	—	—	—	1	2	—	17
Nobles	2	—	—	—	—	—	—	—	0	—	0	0	0	—
Norman	103	—	—	—	2	1	—	—	—	1	4	7	44	37
Pennington	115	—	—	—	2	1	—	—	0	1	4	0	106	1
Pipestone	323	—	—	—	0	1	—	—	—	—	0	1	309	8
Polk	676	—	—	5	3	1	—	—	—	1	9	6	367	37
Pope	6	—	—	—	—	—	—	—	—	—	—	3	0	0
Red Lake	62	—	—	—	1	1	—	—	—	0	2	2	43	5
Redwood	21	—	—	—	—	—	—	—	0	—	0	1	0	—
Renville	18	0	—	—	—	—	—	—	0	—	1	2	0	0
Rock	15	—	—	—	—	—	—	—	—	—	—	4	—	0
Sibley	16	0	—	—	—	—	—	—	—	—	0	1	—	0

Table 11.—Continued

| | | Softwoods | | | | | | | | | | Hardwoods | | |
| | | Northern | | | | | | | | | | | Aspen/ | |
Forest Inventory Unit and county	All species	Eastern redcedar	white-cedar	Balsam fir	Jack pine	Red pine	White pine	Other pine	Spruce	Tama-rack	Total softwoods	Ash	balsam poplar	Bass-wood
Steele	71	--	--	--	--	0	--	--	--	--	0	12	0	6
Stevens	0	--	--	--	--	--	--	--	--	--	--	0	--	--
Swift	9	--	--	--	0	--	--	--	--	--	0	3	--	0
Waseca	27	--	--	--	--	--	--	--	0	0	0	0	--	3
Watonwan	1	--	--	--	--	--	--	--	--	--	--	0	--	--
Wilkin	1	--	--	--	--	--	--	--	--	--	--	--	--	1
Total	3,612	4	--	5	27	15	0	0	4	7	63	108	2,094	182
State total	216,272	32	932	13,073	13,484	14,811	903	356	17,332	4,000	64,924	2,109	114,807	2,748

Hardwoods (continued)

Forest Inventory Unit and county	Beech	White birch	Yellow birch	Black cherry	Black walnut	Cotton-wood	Elm	Hickory	Hard maple	Soft maple	Red oak group	White oak group	Other hardwoods	Total hardwoods
Aspen-Birch Unit														
Carlton	--	252	0	--	--	--	0	0	49	294	73	9	0	3,702
Cook	--	180	--	--	--	--	--	--	0	1	1	--	--	1,216
Koochiching	--	742	0	--	--	--	5	0	29	50	2	9	0	10,267
Lake	--	867	0	--	--	--	0	0	105	579	--	0	0	4,091
St. Louis	--	4,514	62	62	--	--	0	0	496	757	10	0	0	29,700
Total	--	6,555	62	62	--	--	6	6	0	679	1,681	86	19	0	48,978

Table 11.—Continued

<table>
<tr><th rowspan="3">Forest Inventory Unit and county</th><th colspan="14">Hardwoods (continued)</th></tr>
<tr><th rowspan="2">Beech</th><th>White birch</th><th>Yellow birch</th><th>Black cherry</th><th>Black walnut</th><th>Cotton-wood</th><th rowspan="2">Elm</th><th rowspan="2">Hickory</th><th>Hard maple</th><th>Soft maple</th><th>Red oak group</th><th>White oak group</th><th>Other hardwoods</th><th>Total hardwoods</th></tr>
<tr><th>birch</th><th>birch</th><th>cherry</th><th>walnut</th><th>wood</th><th>maple</th><th>maple</th><th>group</th><th>group</th><th>hardwoods</th><th>hardwoods</th></tr>
<tr><td colspan="15">Central Hardwoods Unit</td></tr>
<tr><td>Anoka</td><td>—</td><td>1</td><td>0</td><td>0</td><td>0</td><td>0</td><td>0</td><td>—</td><td>0</td><td>1</td><td>23</td><td>3</td><td>0</td><td>49</td></tr>
<tr><td>Benton</td><td>—</td><td>1</td><td>—</td><td>—</td><td>—</td><td>5</td><td>0</td><td>—</td><td>1</td><td>0</td><td>6</td><td>8</td><td>0</td><td>43</td></tr>
<tr><td>Carver</td><td>—</td><td>—</td><td>—</td><td>—</td><td>—</td><td>26</td><td>1</td><td>—</td><td>3</td><td>0</td><td>11</td><td>11</td><td>7</td><td>59</td></tr>
<tr><td>Chisago</td><td>4</td><td>5</td><td>0</td><td>0</td><td>—</td><td>6</td><td>2</td><td>4</td><td>27</td><td>4</td><td>106</td><td>10</td><td>0</td><td>251</td></tr>
<tr><td>Dakota</td><td>—</td><td>0</td><td>—</td><td>1</td><td>0</td><td>7</td><td>1</td><td>0</td><td>0</td><td>2</td><td>9</td><td>8</td><td>0</td><td>37</td></tr>
<tr><td>Douglas</td><td>—</td><td>1</td><td>—</td><td>—</td><td>0</td><td>268</td><td>4</td><td>—</td><td>2</td><td>1</td><td>10</td><td>14</td><td>1</td><td>346</td></tr>
<tr><td>Fillmore</td><td>—</td><td>0</td><td>—</td><td>8</td><td>47</td><td>2</td><td>38</td><td>12</td><td>75</td><td>9</td><td>306</td><td>165</td><td>0</td><td>762</td></tr>
<tr><td>Goodhue</td><td>—</td><td>2</td><td>—</td><td>5</td><td>22</td><td>4</td><td>10</td><td>3</td><td>44</td><td>20</td><td>182</td><td>53</td><td>1</td><td>505</td></tr>
<tr><td>Hennepin</td><td>—</td><td>—</td><td>—</td><td>1</td><td>2</td><td>1</td><td>1</td><td>0</td><td>11</td><td>1</td><td>29</td><td>16</td><td>5</td><td>101</td></tr>
<tr><td>Houston</td><td>—</td><td>1</td><td>—</td><td>13</td><td>58</td><td>13</td><td>19</td><td>36</td><td>73</td><td>25</td><td>766</td><td>243</td><td>1</td><td>1,349</td></tr>
<tr><td>Isanti</td><td>—</td><td>112</td><td>—</td><td>0</td><td>0</td><td>6</td><td>3</td><td>0</td><td>3</td><td>3</td><td>21</td><td>6</td><td>0</td><td>256</td></tr>
<tr><td>Kanabec</td><td>—</td><td>44</td><td>11</td><td>3</td><td>7</td><td>0</td><td>0</td><td>0</td><td>46</td><td>31</td><td>156</td><td>10</td><td>1</td><td>1,604</td></tr>
<tr><td>Le Sueur</td><td>—</td><td>—</td><td>—</td><td>1</td><td>7</td><td>34</td><td>2</td><td>0</td><td>4</td><td>8</td><td>8</td><td>2</td><td>0</td><td>64</td></tr>
<tr><td>Mille Lacs</td><td>—</td><td>27</td><td>0</td><td>—</td><td>—</td><td>1</td><td>—</td><td>—</td><td>29</td><td>66</td><td>216</td><td>76</td><td>6</td><td>1,501</td></tr>
<tr><td>Morrison</td><td>—</td><td>16</td><td>—</td><td>—</td><td>—</td><td>6</td><td>0</td><td>—</td><td>2</td><td>21</td><td>20</td><td>30</td><td>—</td><td>1,918</td></tr>
<tr><td>Olmsted</td><td>—</td><td>—</td><td>—</td><td>6</td><td>30</td><td>3</td><td>10</td><td>4</td><td>19</td><td>7</td><td>106</td><td>44</td><td>0</td><td>259</td></tr>
<tr><td>Otter Tail</td><td>—</td><td>25</td><td>—</td><td>—</td><td>0</td><td>1</td><td>—</td><td>—</td><td>14</td><td>7</td><td>55</td><td>21</td><td>1</td><td>750</td></tr>
<tr><td>Pine</td><td>13</td><td>424</td><td>0</td><td>0</td><td>0</td><td>0</td><td>0</td><td>13</td><td>270</td><td>1,054</td><td>302</td><td>22</td><td>0</td><td>7,547</td></tr>
<tr><td>Ramsey</td><td>—</td><td>—</td><td>—</td><td>—</td><td>—</td><td>0</td><td>0</td><td>—</td><td>—</td><td>—</td><td>14</td><td>7</td><td>—</td><td>41</td></tr>
<tr><td>Rice</td><td>—</td><td>4</td><td>7</td><td>1</td><td>5</td><td>2</td><td>2</td><td>0</td><td>26</td><td>1</td><td>27</td><td>6</td><td>0</td><td>91</td></tr>
</table>

Table 11.—Continued

Forest Inventory Unit and county	Beech	White birch	Yellow birch	Black cherry	Black walnut	Cotton-wood	Elm	Hickory	Hard maple	Soft maple	Red oak group	White oak group	Other hardwoods	Total hardwoods
						Hardwoods (continued)								
Scott	—	0	—	0	1	60	5	—	3	2	18	15	8	128
Sherburne	—	1	—	0	—	0	0	—	1	2	14	6	0	50
Stearns	—	1	0	2	5	3	2	1	3	3	51	19	0	130
Todd	—	33	12	3	7	182	3	1	40	10	107	61	—	929
Wabasha	—	2	—	9	27	38	15	5	36	47	240	133	1	628
Washington	—	6	—	1	1	0	0	0	0	1	11	9	0	43
Winona	—	2	—	9	46	21	17	12	39	11	372	114	1	718
Wright	—	0	—	0	—	25	1	—	4	1	21	16	0	94
Total	17	705	30	61	267	717	136	91	774	1,328	3,207	1,127	34	20,253
Northern Pine Unit														
Aitkin	—	1,115	0	0	—	1	1	—	161	1,499	639	43	2	12,082
Becker	—	183	11	2	5	9	0	0	165	47	79	6	1	3,579
Beltrami	—	835	—	—	—	13	0	—	178	72	79	12	1	13,025
Cass	—	861	10	2	5	10	0	0	183	417	570	87	1	9,479
Clearwater	—	281	—	0	—	3	0	—	101	33	8	2	0	4,096
Crow Wing	—	205	0	0	—	4	0	—	12	74	122	22	0	3,656
Hubbard	—	577	—	—	—	10	—	—	63	146	56	—	1	7,267
Itasca	—	2,232	21	—	—	5	0	—	152	547	441	27	0	19,177
Lake of the Woods	—	188	—	—	—	3	0	—	5	6	1	1	0	2,725
Mahnomen	—	15	—	—	—	5	0	—	38	2	0	1	—	792

Table 11.—Continued

								Hardwoods (continued)						
Forest Inventory Unit and county	Beech	White birch	Yellow birch	Black cherry	Black walnut	Cotton-wood	Elm	Hickory	Hard maple	Soft maple	Red oak group	White oak group	Other hardwoods	Total hardwoods
Roseau	—	53	—	—	—	4	—	—	6	7	—	0	—	779
Wadena	—	94	—	0	—	6	0	—	11	21	9	6	0	1,912
Total	—	6,639	42	4	10	73	1	1	1,076	2,872	2,004	208	5	78,568
Prairie Unit														
Big Stone	—	—	—	—	—	20	0	—	1	—	—	—	—	21
Blue Earth	—	—	—	0	38	84	3	—	1	5	3	8	2	146
Brown	—	—	—	—	25	78	0	—	1	0	3	1	0	111
Chippewa	—	—	—	—	0	4	1	—	—	—	—	0	—	9
Clay	—	—	—	—	—	5	0	—	0	1	—	3	—	50
Cottonwood	—	—	—	—	2	1	—	—	—	—	—	—	—	4
Dodge	—	—	—	0	8	0	2	0	2	1	0	4	0	19
Faribault	—	—	—	1	9	1	10	4	20	—	87	25	—	185
Freeborn	—	—	—	1	—	38	—	—	—	—	13	10	0	76
Grant	—	—	—	—	0	—	—	—	—	—	0	0	—	1
Jackson	—	—	—	—	0	1	0	—	—	—	—	—	—	1
Kandiyohi	—	—	—	0	2	0	0	—	—	0	0	5	0	15
Kittson	—	11	—	—	—	1	0	—	3	1	—	2	—	872
Lac Qui Parle	—	—	—	—	—	10	0	—	—	—	—	—	—	11
Lincoln	—	—	—	—	0	5	0	—	—	0	—	—	—	7
Lyon	—	—	—	—	1	6	0	—	—	0	—	—	0	9
Marshall	—	13	—	—	—	1	—	—	2	2	—	—	0	393
Martin	—	—	—	—	—	—	0	—	—	—	0	0	—	1

Table 11.—Continued

Forest Inventory Unit and county	Beech	White birch	Yellow birch	Black cherry	Black walnut	Cotton-wood	Elm	Hickory	Hard maple	Soft maple	Red oak group	White oak group	Other hardwoods	Total hardwoods
								Hardwoods (continued)						
McLeod	—	—	—	—	—	—	0	—	—	—	1	1	0	3
Meeker	—	—	—	0	1	—	0	—	—	1	1	4	0	13
Mower	—	—	—	—	2	18	1	—	—	1	6	3	—	40
Murray	—	—	—	—	0	1	—	—	—	—	—	—	—	1
Nicollet	—	—	—	—	19	50	3	—	16	5	2	5	—	119
Nobles	—	—	—	—	0	1	—	—	—	—	—	—	—	1
Norman	—	3	—	—	—	5	1	—	0	1	—	0	—	99
Pennington	—	3	—	—	—	0	—	—	0	0	—	0	—	111
Pipestone	—	—	—	—	1	5	—	—	—	—	—	—	—	323
Polk	—	3	—	0	—	248	0	—	1	2	0	2	—	666
Pope	—	—	—	—	0	—	0	—	—	0	0	2	0	6
Red Lake	—	2	—	—	—	2	—	—	0	0	3	1	1	59
Redwood	—	—	—	—	0	19	—	—	—	—	—	—	—	21
Renville	—	—	—	—	2	10	—	—	0	0	1	1	—	17
Rock	—	—	—	—	1	9	0	—	1	—	—	—	—	15
Sibley	—	—	0	—	3	2	0	0	4	1	1	2	2	16
Steele	—	—	—	1	3	23	4	—	3	0	12	5	—	71
Stevens	—	—	—	—	0	—	—	—	—	0	—	—	—	0
Swift	—	—	—	—	0	1	1	—	—	3	—	0	1	9
Waseca	—	—	—	—	15	—	0	—	2	0	1	4	0	27

Table 11.—Continued

Forest Inventory Unit and county	Hardwoods (continued)													
	Beech	White birch	Yellow birch	Black cherry	Black walnut	Cotton-wood	Elm	Hickory	Hard maple	Soft maple	Red oak group	White oak group	Other hardwoods	Total hardwoods
Watonwan	--	--	--	--	--	--	--	--	--	--	0	--	--	1
Wilkin	--	--	--	--	--	--	--	--	--	--	--	--	--	1
Total	--	35	0	2	136	649	27	4	59	25	133	88	8	3,549
State total	17	13,933	135	67	413	1,445	165	95	2,588	5,906	5,430	1,441	48	151,348

All table cells without observations are indicated by -- . Table value of 0 indicates the volume rounds to less than 1 thousand cubic feet. Columns and rows may not add to their totals due to rounding.

Table 12.—Sawtimber removals from timberland for industrial roundwood, in thousand board feet, International 1/4-inch rule, by Forest Inventory Unit, county, and species group, Minnesota, 2007

Forest Inventory Unit and county	All species	Softwoods										Hardwoods		
		Eastern redcedar	Northern white-cedar	Balsam fir	Jack pine	Red pine	White pine	Other pine	Spruce	Tamarack	Total softwoods	Ash	Aspen/balsam poplar	Basswood
Aspen-Birch Unit														
Carlton	14,668	–	16	821	106	3439	45	77	389	59	4,951	361	7,741	68
Cook	9,696	–	11	476	253	2417	253	193	2196	1	5,799	0	3,043	–
Koochiching	51,661	–	2437	4,167	1717	2771	199	2	9,810	2308	23,409	277	25,742	503
Lake	18,936	–	21	1941	1316	2542	144	37	2463	105	8,569	140	6,732	82
St. Louis	124,326	–	486	9,882	8,510	11,923	825	192	14,792	1944	48,554	945	63,912	223
Total	219,287	–	2970	17,287	11,902	23,091	1465	499	29,651	4,418	91,283	1723	107,170	877
Central Hardwoods Unit														
Anoka	375	0	–	–	2	199	30	–	–	1	232	15	35	1
Benton	286	–	–	–	41	74	–	1	0	3	118	2	63	13
Carver	260	3	–	–	–	–	–	–	–	–	3	5	–	–
Chisago	1158	0	–	–	0	156	36	1	0	0	194	48	168	35
Dakota	138	–	–	–	8	8	10	–	–	–	26	9	5	0
Douglas	1889	–	–	0	1096	1	2	–	0	0	1099	39	29	115
Fillmore	3470	3	–	–	–	6	4	2	3	–	19	149	10	297
Goodhue	2172	5	–	–	–	–	2	–	5	–	12	93	116	443
Hennepin	495	20	–	–	–	3	3	–	–	–	25	100	46	14
Houston	6,021	–	–	–	–	0	–	–	–	–	0	94	69	293
Isanti	1223	0	–	–	41	63	158	0	1	1	264	63	194	17
Kanabec	5,031	1	–	0	3	69	59	–	1	18	152	64	3,327	147
Le Sueur	310	1	–	–	1	1	1	–	1	–	5	19	10	10

Table 12.—Continued

Forest Inventory Unit and county	All species	Softwoods										Hardwoods		
		Eastern redcedar	Northern white-cedar	Balsam fir	Jack pine	Red pine	White pine	Other pine	Spruce	Tamarack	Total softwoods	Ash	Aspen/balsam poplar	Basswood
Mille Lacs	4,734	—	—	—	60	48	41	—	0	12	161	75	2,689	202
Morrison	5,685	0	—	—	92	152	23	3	2	7	279	21	5,055	20
Olmsted	1179	—	—	—	0	4	2	—	0	—	7	46	3	89
Otter Tail	2418	—	—	0	38	58	62	0	0	15	174	59	1629	102
Pine	22,067	4	—	275	305	2060	26	182	86	40	2977	189	14,292	137
Ramsey	212	—	—	—	4	6	4	1	1	—	16	61	38	—
Rice	478	5	—	—	—	—	—	—	—	—	5	21	1	22
Scott	542	5	—	—	—	—	—	—	—	—	5	43	4	10
Sherburne	286	0	—	0	41	91	0	0	0	0	133	41	33	1
Stearns	685	1	—	—	—	119	4	—	1	1	127	35	58	42
Todd	3,682	41	—	14	120	124	23	0	—	17	339	58	1330	294
Wabasha	2932	8	—	—	41	34	—	—	2	—	85	50	37	255
Washington	156	1	—	—	8	4	—	—	—	0	13	33	14	0
Winona	3259	—	—	—	15	36	—	—	0	—	52	78	91	156
Wright	512	8	—	—	62	8	—	—	—	—	77	66	20	37
Total	71,653	106	—	289	1851	3368	574	190	103	116	6,597	1577	29,357	2752
Northern Pine Unit														
Aitkin	40,960	—	4	1056	858	2017	267	19	1228	538	5,986	941	21,296	2373
Becker	14,072	—	—	882	1280	1786	97	20	99	42	4,206	50	8,205	241
Beltrami	48,406	—	118	3,209	2912	2735	300	2	2,838	1139	13,253	216	32,123	359
Cass	51,248	—	8	722	7,632	13,707	979	4	572	465	24,087	294	19,332	1234

Table 12.—Continued

Forest Inventory Unit and county	All species	Softwoods										Hardwoods		
		Eastern redcedar	Northern white-cedar	Balsam fir	Jack pine	Red pine	White pine	Other pine	Spruce	Tama-rack	Total softwoods	Ash	Aspen/balsam poplar	Bass-wood
Clearwater	14,333	--	--	646	118	792	195	1	1015	252	3018	30	9,764	569
Crow Wing	16,517	--	57	85	2146	3790	132	47	63	31	6,352	97	8,633	147
Hubbard	35,030	--	--	1051	5,117	8,645	105	27	531	299	15,774	33	17,364	145
Itasca	86,197	--	80	6,674	7,407	9,615	258	23	7,528	1536	33,122	723	42,640	986
Lake of the Woods	14,776	--	6	688	2992	1069	1	1	1351	1121	7,229	38	7,131	18
Mahnomen	2316	--	--	11	23	74	0	0	0	4	113	27	1875	175
Roseau	4,650	--	--	364	1146	356	0	1	658	79	2604	7	1895	21
Wadena	13,523	--	--	22	4,482	3690	33	1	7	43	8,278	23	4,864	61
Total	342,029	--	273	15,410	36,112	48,274	2368	145	15,891	5,550	124,022	2478	175,122	6,330
Prairie Unit														
Big Stone	101	0	--	--	--	--	--	--	--	--	0	2	--	--
Blue Earth	707	4	--	--	--	3	1	--	--	--	8	12	0	6
Brown	531	0	--	--	--	2	--	--	--	--	2	11	--	5
Chippewa	42	0	--	--	--	0	--	--	--	--	0	15	--	--
Clay	233	--	--	--	--	--	--	--	--	--	--	25	1	168
Cottonwood	23	--	--	--	--	0	0	--	1	--	2	5	--	--
Dodge	100	--	--	--	0	0	0	--	0	--	1	2	3	3
Faribault	838	--	--	--	--	--	--	--	6	--	6	46	--	89
Freeborn	348	--	--	--	--	--	--	--	--	--	--	71	--	--
Grant	3	--	--	--	--	--	--	--	--	--	--	--	--	1
Jackson	8	--	--	--	--	--	--	--	1	--	1	1	--	--

Table 12.—Continued

Forest Inventory Unit and county	All species	Softwoods										Hardwoods		
		Eastern redcedar	Northern white-cedar	Balsam fir	Jack pine	Red pine	White pine	Other pine	Spruce	Tama-rack	Total softwoods	Ash	Aspen/ balsam poplar	Bass-wood
Kandiyohi	60	6	--	--	--	--	--	--	--	--	6	23	0	4
Kittson	2408	--	--	0	19	13	--	0	0	5	38	2	2319	4
Lac Qui Parle	52	0	--	--	--	--	--	--	--	--	0	2	--	--
Lincoln	31	--	--	--	--	0	--	--	--	--	0	5	--	--
Lyon	45	--	--	--	--	0	--	--	1	--	2	9	0	--
Marshall	1102	--	--	0	24	16	0	0	0	6	47	1	1018	6
Martin	3	--	--	--	--	--	--	--	--	--	--	2	--	--
McLeod	12	--	--	--	--	--	--	--	--	--	--	2	0	0
Meeker	60	3	--	--	--	--	--	--	--	--	3	18	0	5
Mower	183	--	--	--	--	--	--	--	--	--	--	37	--	0
Murray	9	--	--	--	--	--	--	--	2	--	2	1	0	--
Nicollet	604	2	--	--	--	--	--	--	--	--	2	9	--	97
Nobles	8	--	--	--	--	--	--	--	1	--	1	1	--	--
Norman	373	--	--	--	6	4	--	--	--	1	11	31	121	172
Pennington	309	--	--	--	4	3	--	--	0	1	9	1	291	1
Pipestone	888	--	--	--	0	--	--	--	--	--	0	4	844	14
Polk	2415	--	--	12	6	4	--	--	--	2	23	28	1005	170
Pope	13	--	--	--	--	--	--	--	--	--	--	5	0	1
Red Lake	189	--	--	--	3	2	--	--	--	1	6	10	118	21
Redwood	97	--	--	--	--	--	--	--	0	--	0	3	0	0
Renville	85	2	--	--	--	--	--	--	2	--	4	11	1	1

Table 12.—Continued

Forest Inventory Unit and county	Softwoods											Hardwoods		
	All species	Eastern redcedar	Northern white-cedar	Balsam fir	Jack pine	Red pine	White pine	Other pine	Spruce	Tama-rack	Total softwoods	Ash	Aspen/ balsam poplar	Bass-wood
Rock	71	—	—	—	—	—	—	—	—	—	—	17	—	—
Sibley	81	1	—	—	—	—	—	—	—	—	1	3	—	0
Steele	327	—	—	—	—	1	—	—	—	—	1	58	1	30
Stevens	1	—	—	—	—	—	—	—	—	—	—	0	—	—
Swift	30	—	—	—	0	—	—	—	—	—	0	8	—	0
Waseca	131	—	—	—	—	—	—	—	1	—	1	1	—	13
Watonwan	3	—	—	—	—	—	—	—	—	—	—	1	—	—
Wilkin	7	—	—	—	—	—	—	—	—	—	—	—	—	7
Total	12,529	18	—	12	63	50	2	0	16	17	178	479	5,724	820
State total	645,497	124	3243	32,998	49,928	74,783	4409	834	45,661	10,100	222,079	6,258	317,374	10,780

Table 12.—Continued

Forest Inventory Unit and county	Beech	White birch	Yellow birch	Black cherry	Black walnut	Cotton-wood	Elm	Hickory	Hard maple	Soft maple	Red oak group	White oak group	Other hardwoods	Total hardwoods
Aspen-Birch Unit														
Carlton	–	666	0	–	–	0	0	–	85	499	281	17	0	9,717
Cook	–	851	–	–	–	–	–	–	0	2	2	–	–	3,897
Koochiching	–	1515	0	–	–	9	0	–	69	87	10	38	0	28,252
Lake	–	2248	1	–	–	0	0	–	164	999	–	0	0	10,366
St. Louis	–	8,729	107	–	–	0	0	–	567	1244	43	1	0	75,772
Total	–	14,009	108	–	–	10	1	–	885	2,831	335	56	0	128,004
Central Hardwoods Unit														
Anoka	–	2	0	0	0	1	1	–	1	1	81	5	0	143
Benton	–	2	–	–	–	22	0	–	4	0	28	34	0	168
Carver	–	–	–	–	–	121	3	–	13	0	40	43	32	257
Chisago	20	8	0	1	–	30	11	20	121	16	450	36	1	964
Dakota	–	1	–	4	1	26	2	1	1	5	29	28	1	112
Douglas	–	1	–	–	2	465	20	–	9	5	44	58	3	791
Fillmore	–	1	–	41	231	12	181	57	354	43	1319	757	0	3451
Goodhue	–	3	–	24	109	19	47	14	210	65	784	229	3	2159
Hennepin	–	–	–	3	9	7	5	1	51	3	134	73	24	469
Houston	–	4	–	62	278	62	88	170	345	118	3297	1136	4	6,021
Isanti	–	524	–	0	0	30	16	0	9	10	77	17	1	959
Kanabec	–	116	63	15	41	0	1	2	231	77	754	37	4	4,879

Table 12.—Continued

Forest Inventory Unit and county	Beech	White birch	Yellow birch	Black cherry	Black walnut	Cotton-wood	Elm	Hickory	Hard maple	Soft maple	Red oak group	White oak group	Other hardwoods	Total hardwoods
							Hardwoods (continued)							
Le Sueur	--	--	--	3	40	158	7	0	19	4	33	10	0	305
Mille Lacs	--	80	0	--	--	3	--	--	85	160	927	325	27	4,573
Morrison	--	27	--	--	--	25	0	--	2	39	86	130	--	5,406
Olmsted	--	--	--	30	148	16	48	19	91	33	458	192	0	1173
Otter Tail	--	49	--	--	1	3	--	--	49	22	235	92	5	2244
Pine	60	600	0	2	2	0	0	60	547	1,829	1283	88	1	19,090
Ramsey	--	--	--	--	1	0	1	--	--	--	64	31	--	196
Rice	--	25	41	4	27	11	10	1	144	3	140	25	1	473
Scott	--	1	--	2	2	278	22	--	14	6	63	56	36	537
Sherburne	--	1	--	0	--	1	1	--	5	5	44	20	1	153
Stearns	--	3	1	10	27	15	8	3	16	12	249	80	1	558
Todd	--	128	66	14	41	325	15	3	215	44	551	258	--	3342
Wabasha	--	9	--	44	131	178	70	24	169	219	1033	621	9	2847
Washington	--	11	--	3	2	1	1	1	0	3	38	34	2	143
Winona	--	7	--	46	223	99	79	54	181	51	1600	539	3	3207
Wright	--	0	--	0	--	119	4	--	18	3	96	71	1	435
Total	80	1602	171	307	1318	2024	638	427	2905	2,776	13,937	5,023	160	65,056
Northern Pine Unit														
Aitkin	--	3,989	2	0	--	1	2	--	527	2,920	2739	178	8	34,975
Becker	--	343	50	10	29	30	1	2	376	93	404	27	3	9,865
Beltrami	--	1602	--	--	--	23	0	--	309	125	341	52	3	35,153

94

Table 12.—Continued

Forest Inventory Unit and county	Beech	White birch	Yellow birch	Black cherry	Black walnut	Cotton-wood	Elm	Hickory	Hard maple	Soft maple	Red oak group	White oak group	Other hardwoods	Total hardwoods
Cass	—	2151	50	10	29	17	0	2	416	729	2516	375	5	27,161
Clearwater	—	672	—	0	—	5	0	0	176	57	32	10	0	11,315
Crow Wing	—	476	0	0	—	15	0	—	37	141	524	95	0	10,165
Hubbard	—	1089	—	—	—	18	—	—	109	254	241	—	3	19,257
Itasca	—	5,263	37	—	—	8	0	—	462	945	1898	114	0	53,076
Lake of the Woods	—	328	—	—	—	5	0	—	9	12	2	4	0	7,546
Mahnomen	—	27	—	—	—	24	0	—	67	3	1	6	—	2203
Roseau	—	91	—	—	—	6	—	—	10	13	—	2	—	2046
Wadena	—	163	—	0	—	11	0	—	23	41	36	22	0	5,245
Total	—	16,195	138	21	57	164	4	4	2,521	5,333	8,733	883	24	218,007
Prairie Unit														
Big Stone	—	—	—	—	—	94	1	—	5	—	—	—	—	101
Blue Earth	—	—	—	0	193	394	13	—	6	21	11	35	7	699
Brown	—	—	—	—	123	364	2	—	4	2	12	6	0	529
Chippewa	—	—	—	—	2	20	5	—	—	—	—	0	—	41
Clay	—	—	—	—	—	23	1	—	1	3	—	11	—	233
Cottonwood	—	—	—	—	12	4	—	—	—	—	—	—	—	21
Dodge	—	—	—	2	38	1	10	0	12	3	1	22	2	99
Faribault	—	—	—	2	43	5	45	18	95	—	381	108	—	833
Freeborn	—	—	—	3	—	177	—	—	—	—	54	41	1	348
Grant	—	—	—	1	—	—	—	—	—	—	1	1	—	3

Table 12.—Continued

Forest Inventory Unit and county		Hardwoods (continued)												
	Beech	White birch	Yellow birch	Black cherry	Black walnut	Cotton-wood	Elm	Hickory	Hard maple	Soft maple	Red oak group	White oak group	Other hardwoods	Total hardwoods
Jackson	—	—	—	—	2	4	—	—	—	—	—	—	—	7
Kandiyohi	—	—	—	0	8	0	0	—	—	0	1	18	0	55
Kittson	—	18	—	—	—	1	0	—	13	3	—	9	—	2370
Lac Qui Parle	—	—	—	—	—	49	1	—	—	—	—	—	—	52
Lincoln	—	—	—	—	2	23	0	—	—	0	—	—	—	31
Lyon	—	—	—	—	5	27	0	—	—	1	—	—	2	44
Marshall	—	23	—	—	—	2	—	—	3	3	1	—	—	1055
Martin	—	—	—	—	—	—	0	—	—	—	—	0	—	3
McLeod	—	—	—	—	—	—	1	—	—	—	4	4	0	12
Meeker	—	—	—	1	5	—	2	—	—	5	4	16	1	57
Mower	—	—	—	—	9	86	6	—	—	5	27	13	—	183
Murray	—	—	—	—	2	4	—	—	—	—	—	—	—	7
Nicollet	—	—	—	—	106	236	14	—	88	21	7	24	—	602
Nobles	—	—	—	—	2	4	—	—	—	—	—	—	—	7
Norman	—	5	—	—	—	23	3	—	1	4	—	1	—	362
Pennington	—	4	—	—	—	0	—	—	1	1	—	1	—	300
Pipestone	—	—	—	—	3	23	—	—	—	—	—	—	—	887
Polk	—	6	—	0	—	1163	1	—	3	5	0	11	—	2392
Pope	—	—	—	—	1	—	0	—	—	1	1	3	1	13
Red Lake	—	3	—	—	—	7	—	—	0	0	12	4	7	183

Table 12.—Continued

	Hardwoods (continued)													
Forest Inventory Unit and county	Beech	White birch	Yellow birch	Black cherry	Black walnut	Cotton-wood	Elm	Hickory	Hard maple	Soft maple	Red oak group	White oak group	Other hardwoods	Total hardwoods
Redwood	–	–	–	–	2	91	–	–	–	–	–	–	–	97
Renville	–	–	–	–	12	47	–	–	2	0	2	5	–	81
Rock	–	–	–	–	6	44	0	–	4	–	–	–	–	71
Sibley	–	–	0	–	20	10	2	0	20	4	3	8	10	80
Steele	–	–	–	3	16	108	18	–	16	1	53	21	–	325
Stevens	–	–	–	–	0	–	–	–	–	0	–	–	–	1
Swift	–	–	–	–	0	4	2	–	–	12	–	0	2	29
Waseca	–	–	–	–	77	–	0	–	13	2	4	19	1	130
Watonwan	–	–	–	–	–	–	–	–	–	–	1	–	–	3
Wilkin	–	–	–	–	–	–	–	–	–	–	–	–	–	7
Total	–	60	0	11	691	3040	127	18	285	98	581	382	35	12,351
State total	80	31,865	417	339	2066	5,238	769	450	6,596	11,038	23,585	6,344	219	423,418

97

Table 13.—Harvest residue generated by industrial roundwood harvesting, in thousand cubic feet, by Forest Inventory Unit, county, and species group. Minnesota, 2007

Forest Inventory Unit and county	All species	Softwoods										Hardwoods		
		Eastern redcedar	Northern white-cedar	Balsam fir	Jack pine	Red pine	White pine	Other pine	Spruce	Tamarack	Total softwoods	Ash	Aspen/balsam poplar	Basswood
Aspen-Birch Unit														
Carlton	2,290	—	3	178	9	272	3	17	82	6	571	77	1,267	16
Cook	1,360	—	2	79	38	193	19	42	373	0	747	0	498	—
Koochiching	9,146	—	355	895	291	227	15	0	2,059	396	4,239	37	4,323	76
Lake	3,365	—	3	409	208	219	12	8	510	12	1,381	19	1,100	27
St. Louis	21,918	—	87	2,083	1,546	1,041	66	42	3,027	382	8,273	186	10,616	40
Total	38,078	—	449	3,644	2,093	1,952	114	109	6,051	798	15,211	319	17,805	159
Central Hardwoods Unit														
Anoka	43	0	—	—	0	15	2	—	—	0	18	1	5	0
Benton	36	—	—	—	3	5	—	0	0	0	8	0	8	2
Carver	43	0	—	—	—	—	—	—	—	—	0	1	—	—
Chisago	198	0	—	—	0	12	3	0	0	0	14	6	28	5
Dakota	19	—	—	—	1	1	1	—	—	—	2	1	0	0
Douglas	366	—	—	0	158	0	0	—	0	0	158	5	5	16
Fillmore	648	0	—	—	—	0	0	0	0	—	2	21	2	41
Goodhue	399	1	—	—	—	—	0	—	1	—	2	16	20	61
Hennepin	52	1	—	—	—	0	0	—	—	—	2	6	2	1
Houston	1,208	—	—	—	0	0	—	—	—	—	0	13	11	40
Isanti	140	0	—	—	3	5	12	0	0	0	20	6	19	2
Kanabec	814	0	—	0	1	6	4	—	0	1	12	7	563	36
Le Sueur	43	0	—	—	0	0	0	—	0	—	1	3	—	1

Table 13.—Continued

Forest Inventory Unit and county	All species	Softwoods										Hardwoods		
		Eastern redcedar	Northern white-cedar	Balsam fir	Jack pine	Red pine	White pine	Other pine	Spruce	Tama-rack	Total softwoods	Ash	Aspen/ balsam poplar	Bass-wood
Mille Lacs	850	—	—	—	9	4	3	—	0	1	17	11	428	29
Morrison	904	0	—	—	7	10	2	1	1	1	22	2	802	3
Olmsted	217	—	—	—	0	0	0	—	0	—	0	6	0	12
Otter Tail	427	—	—	0	8	6	5	0	0	3	22	9	276	16
Pine	3,876	1	—	35	53	184	2	40	18	6	339	27	2,335	28
Ramsey	13	—	—	—	0	0	0	0	0	—	1	3	2	—
Rice	53	1	—	—	—	—	—	—	—	—	1	3	0	3
Scott	82	1	—	—	—	—	—	—	—	—	1	6	0	1
Sherburne	21	0	—	0	3	6	0	0	0	0	9	2	3	0
Stearns	90	0	—	—	—	8	0	—	0	0	9	4	10	6
Todd	530	6	—	2	12	9	2	0	—	3	33	8	160	42
Wabasha	534	1	—	—	—	5	3	—	0	—	9	7	6	35
Washington	20	0	—	—	—	1	0	—	—	0	1	2	1	0
Winona	629	—	—	—	1	1	5	—	0	—	6	11	14	22
Wright	66	0	—	—	4	1	—	—	—	—	5	6	1	5
Total	12,322	13	—	37	257	282	45	41	21	16	712	191	4,702	408
Northern Pine Unit														
Aitkin	7,154	—	1	208	120	152	20	4	243	33	781	153	3,538	384
Becker	2,285	—	—	174	192	142	11	4	22	9	555	8	1,393	38
Beltrami	8,460	—	17	670	481	229	31	0	557	215	2,200	32	5,444	64
Cass	7,474	—	1	134	1,120	1,042	76	1	105	46	2,524	40	3,254	183

Table 13.—Continued

Forest Inventory Unit and county	All species	Softwoods										Hardwoods		
		Eastern redcedar	Northern white-cedar	Balsam fir	Jack pine	Red pine	White pine	Other pine	Spruce	Tamarack	Total softwoods	Ash	Aspen/balsam poplar	Basswood
Clearwater	2,442	—	—	128	25	77	26	0	172	22	450	5	1,653	82
Crow Wing	2,458	—	9	19	304	282	11	10	14	5	653	12	1,451	30
Hubbard	5,269	—	—	194	765	676	12	6	91	33	1,776	7	2,943	32
Itasca	14,549	—	11	1,355	1,132	743	20	5	1,492	237	4,995	100	7,167	149
Lake of the Woods	2,539	—	1	148	489	83	0	0	268	229	1,217	6	1,194	6
Mahnomen	403	—	—	2	5	11	0	0	0	1	19	4	318	25
Roseau	782	—	—	57	179	42	0	0	118	15	411	2	322	7
Wadena	1,870	—	—	5	661	287	4	0	1	10	969	5	792	16
Total	55,685	—	40	3,092	5,473	3,766	212	32	3,082	855	16,551	373	29,469	1,014
Prairie Unit														
Big Stone	14	0	—	—	—	—	—	—	—	—	0	0	—	—
Blue Earth	96	1	—	—	—	0	0	—	—	—	1	2	0	1
Brown	72	0	—	—	—	0	—	—	—	—	0	2	—	1
Chippewa	6	0	—	—	—	0	—	—	—	—	0	2	—	—
Clay	33	—	—	—	—	—	—	—	—	—	—	3	0	23
Cottonwood	3	—	—	—	—	0	0	—	0	—	0	1	—	—
Dodge	10	—	—	—	0	0	0	—	0	—	0	0	0	0
Faribault	157	—	—	—	—	—	—	—	1	—	1	6	—	12
Freeborn	57	—	—	—	—	—	—	—	—	—	—	10	—	—
Grant	1	—	—	—	—	—	—	—	0	—	0	—	—	—
Jackson	1	—	—	—	—	—	—	—	—	—	0	0	—	—

Table 13.—Continued

Forest Inventory Unit and county	All species	Softwoods										Hardwoods		
		Eastern redcedar	Northern white-cedar	Balsam fir	Jack pine	Red pine	White pine	Other pine	Spruce	Tama-rack	Total softwoods	Ash	Aspen/ balsam poplar	Bass-wood
Kandiyohi	9	1	—	—	—	—	—	—	—	—	1	3	0	0
Kittson	414	—	—	0	4	2	—	0	0	1	7	0	394	1
Lac Qui Parle	7	0	—	—	—	—	—	—	—	—	0	0	—	—
Lincoln	4	—	—	—	—	0	—	—	—	—	0	1	—	—
Lyon	6	—	—	—	—	0	—	—	0	—	0	1	0	—
Marshall	194	—	—	0	5	2	0	0	0	1	9	0	173	2
Martin	0	—	—	—	—	—	—	—	—	—	—	0	—	—
McLeod	2	—	—	—	—	—	—	—	—	—	—	0	0	0
Meeker	10	0	—	—	—	—	—	—	—	—	0	3	0	1
Mower	29	—	—	—	—	—	—	—	—	—	—	5	—	0
Murray	1	—	—	—	—	—	—	—	0	—	0	0	0	—
Nicollet	69	0	—	—	—	—	—	—	—	—	0	1	—	8
Nobles	1	—	—	—	—	—	—	—	0	—	0	0	—	—
Norman	58	—	—	—	1	1	—	—	—	0	2	4	21	24
Pennington	54	—	—	—	1	0	—	—	0	0	2	0	49	0
Pipestone	152	—	—	—	0	—	—	—	—	—	0	1	143	5
Polk	370	—	—	3	1	1	—	—	—	0	5	4	171	24
Pope	1	—	—	—	—	—	—	—	—	—	—	0	0	0
Red Lake	33	—	—	—	1	0	—	—	—	0	1	1	20	3
Redwood	13	—	—	—	—	—	—	—	0	—	0	0	0	—
Renville	11	0	—	—	—	—	—	—	0	—	1	1	0	0

Table 13.—Continued

Forest Inventory Unit and county	Softwoods											Hardwoods		
	All species	Eastern redcedar	Northern white-cedar	Balsam fir	Jack pine	Red pine	White pine	Other pine	Spruce	Tamarack	Total softwoods	Ash	Aspen/balsam poplar	Basswood
Rock	10	—	—	—	—	—	—	—	—	—	—	2	—	—
Sibley	9	0	—	—	—	—	—	—	—	—	0	0	0	0
Steele	52	—	—	—	—	0	—	—	—	—	0	8	0	4
Stevens	0	—	—	—	—	—	—	—	—	—	—	0	—	—
Swift	4	—	—	—	0	—	—	—	—	—	0	1	—	0
Waseca	18	—	—	—	—	—	—	—	0	—	0	0	—	2
Watonwan	1	—	—	—	—	—	—	—	—	—	—	0	—	—
Wilkin	1	—	—	—	—	—	—	—	—	—	—	—	—	1
Total	1,984	3	—	3	14	7	0	0	2	4	32	66	971	113
State total	108,069	15	489	6,776	7,837	6,008	371	182	9,156	1,672	32,506	949	52,947	1,694

Table 13.—Continued

<table>
<thead>
<tr><th rowspan="2">Forest Inventory Unit and county</th><th colspan="14">Hardwoods (continued)</th></tr>
<tr><th>Beech</th><th>White birch</th><th>Yellow birch</th><th>Black cherry</th><th>Black walnut</th><th>Cotton-wood</th><th>Elm</th><th>Hickory</th><th>Hard maple</th><th>Soft maple</th><th>Red oak group</th><th>White oak group</th><th>Other hardwoods</th><th>Total hardwoods</th></tr>
</thead>
<tbody>
<tr><td colspan="15">Aspen-Birch Unit</td></tr>
<tr><td>Carlton</td><td>--</td><td>114</td><td>0</td><td>--</td><td>--</td><td>0</td><td>0</td><td>--</td><td>14</td><td>159</td><td>67</td><td>5</td><td>0</td><td>1,719</td></tr>
<tr><td>Cook</td><td>--</td><td>114</td><td>--</td><td>--</td><td>--</td><td>--</td><td>--</td><td>--</td><td>0</td><td>1</td><td>--</td><td>--</td><td>--</td><td>613</td></tr>
<tr><td>Koochiching</td><td>--</td><td>412</td><td>0</td><td>--</td><td>--</td><td>3</td><td>0</td><td>--</td><td>17</td><td>27</td><td>2</td><td>9</td><td>0</td><td>4,906</td></tr>
<tr><td>Lake</td><td>--</td><td>467</td><td>0</td><td>--</td><td>--</td><td>0</td><td>0</td><td>--</td><td>46</td><td>325</td><td>--</td><td>0</td><td>0</td><td>1,984</td></tr>
<tr><td>St. Louis</td><td>--</td><td>2,269</td><td>35</td><td>--</td><td>--</td><td>0</td><td>0</td><td>--</td><td>112</td><td>377</td><td>10</td><td>0</td><td>0</td><td>13,645</td></tr>
<tr><td>Total</td><td>--</td><td>3,376</td><td>35</td><td>--</td><td>--</td><td>3</td><td>0</td><td>--</td><td>189</td><td>888</td><td>80</td><td>14</td><td>0</td><td>22,867</td></tr>
<tr><td colspan="15">Central Hardwoods Unit</td></tr>
<tr><td>Anoka</td><td>--</td><td>1</td><td>0</td><td>0</td><td>0</td><td>0</td><td>0</td><td>--</td><td>0</td><td>0</td><td>17</td><td>0</td><td>0</td><td>25</td></tr>
<tr><td>Benton</td><td>--</td><td>0</td><td>--</td><td>--</td><td>--</td><td>3</td><td>0</td><td>--</td><td>1</td><td>0</td><td>6</td><td>8</td><td>0</td><td>29</td></tr>
<tr><td>Carver</td><td>--</td><td>--</td><td>--</td><td>--</td><td>--</td><td>17</td><td>0</td><td>--</td><td>2</td><td>0</td><td>9</td><td>9</td><td>4</td><td>42</td></tr>
<tr><td>Chisago</td><td>3</td><td>3</td><td>0</td><td>0</td><td>--</td><td>4</td><td>2</td><td>3</td><td>17</td><td>2</td><td>104</td><td>8</td><td>0</td><td>184</td></tr>
<tr><td>Dakota</td><td>--</td><td>0</td><td>--</td><td>1</td><td>--</td><td>3</td><td>0</td><td>0</td><td>0</td><td>1</td><td>6</td><td>6</td><td>0</td><td>17</td></tr>
<tr><td>Douglas</td><td>--</td><td>0</td><td>--</td><td>--</td><td>--</td><td>152</td><td>3</td><td>--</td><td>1</td><td>1</td><td>10</td><td>13</td><td>0</td><td>207</td></tr>
<tr><td>Fillmore</td><td>--</td><td>0</td><td>--</td><td>5</td><td>29</td><td>2</td><td>25</td><td>8</td><td>49</td><td>6</td><td>306</td><td>154</td><td>0</td><td>646</td></tr>
<tr><td>Goodhue</td><td>--</td><td>1</td><td>--</td><td>3</td><td>12</td><td>3</td><td>6</td><td>2</td><td>27</td><td>12</td><td>182</td><td>52</td><td>0</td><td>397</td></tr>
<tr><td>Hennepin</td><td>--</td><td>--</td><td>--</td><td>0</td><td>1</td><td>1</td><td>1</td><td>0</td><td>7</td><td>0</td><td>16</td><td>11</td><td>3</td><td>50</td></tr>
<tr><td>Houston</td><td>--</td><td>1</td><td>--</td><td>8</td><td>37</td><td>9</td><td>12</td><td>23</td><td>47</td><td>16</td><td>767</td><td>224</td><td>1</td><td>1,208</td></tr>
<tr><td>Isanti</td><td>--</td><td>71</td><td>--</td><td>0</td><td>0</td><td>4</td><td>2</td><td>0</td><td>1</td><td>1</td><td>13</td><td>2</td><td>0</td><td>121</td></tr>
<tr><td>Kanabec</td><td>--</td><td>24</td><td>5</td><td>1</td><td>3</td><td>0</td><td>0</td><td>0</td><td>22</td><td>17</td><td>115</td><td>7</td><td>1</td><td>802</td></tr>
<tr><td>Le Sueur</td><td>--</td><td>--</td><td>--</td><td>0</td><td>4</td><td>22</td><td>1</td><td>0</td><td>2</td><td>1</td><td>8</td><td>2</td><td>0</td><td>43</td></tr>
</tbody>
</table>

Table 13.—Continued

Forest Inventory Unit and county	Hardwoods (continued)													
	Beech	White birch	Yellow birch	Black cherry	Black walnut	Cotton-wood	Elm	Hickory	Hard maple	Soft maple	Red oak group	White oak group	Other hardwoods	Total hardwoods
Mille Lacs	—	15	0	—	—	0	—	—	16	39	215	75	4	834
Morrison	—	9	—	—	—	4	0	—	1	12	20	30	—	882
Olmsted	—	—	—	3	18	2	6	2	12	4	106	43	0	216
Otter Tail	—	14	—	—	0	1	—	—	9	4	55	21	1	404
Pine	8	149	0	0	0	0	0	8	81	582	297	20	0	3,536
Ramsey	—	—	—	—	0	0	0	—	—	—	5	2	—	12
Rice	—	2	3	0	3	2	1	0	12	0	16	6	0	52
Scott	—	0	—	0	0	38	3	—	2	1	13	12	5	82
Sherburne	—	0	—	0	—	0	0	—	0	0	3	1	0	12
Stearns	—	0	0	1	2	2	1	0	1	1	35	18	0	82
Todd	—	19	5	1	3	104	2	0	19	6	68	59	—	497
Wabasha	—	1	—	5	17	25	9	3	23	30	240	122	1	525
Washington	—	3	—	0	0	0	0	0	0	0	5	6	0	19
Winona	—	1	—	5	29	14	11	7	25	7	372	105	0	623
Wright	—	0	—	0	—	16	0	—	2	0	16	14	0	62
Total	11	315	13	35	159	427	85	58	380	744	3,027	1,031	22	11,610
Northern Pine Unit														
Aitkin	—	672	0	0	0	0	0	—	90	856	636	41	1	6,373
Becker	—	103	5	1	2	6	0	0	91	27	52	4	0	1,730
Beltrami	—	478	—	—	—	7	0	—	101	41	79	12	0	6,260
Cass	—	495	5	1	2	5	0	0	101	235	542	87	1	4,950

104

Table 13.—Continued

									Hardwoods (continued)					
Forest Inventory Unit and county	Beech	White birch	Yellow birch	Black cherry	Black walnut	Cotton-wood	Elm	Hickory	Hard maple	Soft maple	Red oak group	White oak group	Other hardwoods	Total hardwoods
Clearwater	—	165	—	0	—	2	0	—	57	19	8	2	0	1,992
Crow Wing	—	117	0	0	—	3	0	—	7	42	122	22	0	1,805
Hubbard	—	330	—	—	—	6	—	—	36	83	56	—	0	3,493
Itasca	—	1,265	12	—	—	3	0	—	86	306	441	26	0	9,554
Lake of the Woods	—	106	—	—	—	2	0	—	3	4	1	1	0	1,322
Mahnomen	—	9	—	—	—	4	0	—	21	1	0	1	—	383
Roseau	—	30	—	—	—	2	—	—	3	4	—	0	—	371
Wadena	—	53	—	—	0	4	0	—	7	12	8	5	0	901
Total	—	3,824	22	2	4	43	0	0	603	1,630	1,944	201	3	39,134
Prairie Unit														
Big Stone	—	—	—	—	—	13	0	—	0	—	—	—	—	14
Blue Earth	—	—	—	—	0	55	2	—	1	3	3	7	1	95
Brown	—	—	—	—	15	50	0	—	0	0	3	1	0	72
Chippewa	—	—	—	—	—	3	1	—	—	—	—	0	—	6
Clay	—	—	—	—	—	3	0	—	0	0	—	3	—	33
Cottonwood	—	—	—	—	1	1	—	—	—	—	—	—	—	2
Dodge	—	—	—	—	4	0	1	0	1	0	0	2	0	10
Faribault	—	—	—	—	5	1	6	2	13	—	85	25	—	157
Freeborn	—	—	—	—	—	24	—	—	—	—	13	10	0	57
Grant	—	—	—	—	0	—	—	—	—	—	—	0	—	1
Jackson	—	—	—	—	0	1	—	—	—	—	—	—	—	1

Table 13.—Continued

	Hardwoods (continued)													
Forest Inventory Unit and county	Beech	White birch	Yellow birch	Black cherry	Black walnut	Cotton-wood	Elm	Hickory	Hard maple	Soft maple	Red oak group	White oak group	Other hardwoods	Total hardwoods
Kandiyohi	—	—	—	0	1	0	0	—	—	0	0	4	0	9
Kittson	—	6	—	—	—	0	0	—	2	1	—	2	—	406
Lac Qui Parle	—	—	—	—	—	7	0	—	—	—	—	—	—	7
Lincoln	—	—	—	—	0	3	0	—	—	0	—	—	—	4
Lyon	—	—	—	—	1	4	0	—	—	0	—	—	0	6
Marshall	—	7	—	—	—	1	—	—	1	1	—	—	—	185
Martin	—	—	—	—	—	—	0	—	—	—	0	0	—	0
McLeod	—	—	—	—	—	—	0	—	—	—	1	1	0	2
Meeker	—	—	—	0	1	—	0	—	—	1	1	4	0	10
Mower	—	—	—	—	1	12	1	—	—	1	6	3	—	29
Murray	—	—	—	—	0	1	—	—	—	—	—	—	—	1
Nicollet	—	—	—	—	9	33	2	—	7	3	2	5	—	69
Nobles	—	—	—	—	0	1	0	—	—	—	—	—	—	1
Norman	—	2	—	—	—	3	0	—	0	1	—	0	—	56
Pennington	—	1	—	—	—	0	—	—	0	0	—	0	—	52
Pipestone	—	—	—	—	0	3	—	—	—	—	—	—	—	152
Polk	—	2	—	0	—	161	0	—	1	1	0	2	—	366
Pope	—	—	—	—	0	—	0	—	—	0	0	0	0	1
Red Lake	—	1	—	—	—	1	—	—	0	0	3	1	1	32
Redwood	—	—	—	—	0	13	—	—	—	0	—	—	—	13
Renville	—	—	—	—	1	6	—	—	0	0	1	0	—	10

Table 13.—Continued

Forest Inventory Unit and county	Hardwoods (continued)															
	Beech	White birch	Yellow birch	Black cherry	Black walnut	Cotton-wood	Elm	Hickory	Hard maple	Soft maple	Red oak group	White oak group	Other hardwoods	Total hardwoods
Rock	--	--	--	--	1	6	0	--	1	--	--	--	--	10
Sibley	--	--	0	--	2	1	0	0	2	1	1	1	1	9
Steele	--	--	--	0	2	15	2	--	2	0	12	5	--	52
Stevens	--	--	--	--	0	--	--	--	--	0	--	--	--	0
Swift	--	--	--	--	0	1	0	--	--	2	--	0	0	3
Waseca	--	--	--	--	9	--	0	--	1	0	1	4	0	18
Watonwan	--	--	--	--	--	--	--	--	--	--	0	--	--	1
Wilkin	--	--	--	--	--	--	--	--	--	--	--	--	--	1
Total	--	20	0	1	76	421	16	3	32	15	131	81	5	1,952
State total	11	7,535	70	38	240	894	102	61	1,205	3,278	5,182	1,328	30	75,563

All table cells without observations are indicated by --. Table value of 0 indicates the volume rounds to less than 1 thousand cubic feet. Columns and rows may not add to their totals due to rounding.

Table 14.—Disposition of residues produced at primary wood-using mills, in thousand tons, green weight, by Forest Inventory Unit, disposition, residue type, and softwoods and hardwoods, Minnesota, 2007

(In thousand tons, green weight)

Forest Inventory Unit and disposition	Total all residues		Residue type							
			Total wood residue		Wood residue				Bark	
					Coarse[a]		Fine[b]			
	Softwood	Hardwood	Softwood	Hardwood	Softwood	Hardwood	Softwood	Hardwood	Softwood	Hardwood
All Units										
Fiber products	145.19	23.11	145.19	23.11	144.65	23.02	0.54	0.09	—	—
Industrial fuel	243.62	694.38	96.63	204.63	26.69	25.02	69.95	179.61	146.99	489.75
Residential fuel	28.02	91.12	23.38	62.98	19.95	53.34	3.43	9.64	4.64	28.14
Mulch	26.20	11.10	8.46	6.19	7.38	5.54	1.08	0.65	17.74	4.91
Animal bedding	87.61	34.60	87.18	31.00	0.29	6.35	86.89	24.65	0.43	3.60
Miscellaneous[c]	28.93	57.66	21.46	38.09	13.90	18.82	7.56	19.27	7.47	19.57
Not used	3.92	12.65	2.13	9.58	0.47	1.83	1.67	7.75	1.79	3.07
State total	563.51	924.62	384.44	375.58	213.32	133.91	171.12	241.67	179.07	549.04
Aspen-Birch										
Fiber products	5.10	8.23	5.10	8.23	4.56	8.13	0.54	0.09	—	—
Industrial fuel	99.62	386.50	41.21	117.65	7.96	4.21	33.25	113.45	58.41	268.85
Residential fuel	10.49	24.89	9.22	7.64	8.12	3.92	1.10	3.72	1.27	17.25
Mulch	10.55	5.00	7.36	3.60	7.09	3.53	0.27	0.07	3.19	1.40
Animal bedding	7.90	6.39	7.82	6.35	0.01	0.00	7.81	6.35	0.08	0.04
Miscellaneous[c]	12.51	13.12	8.42	6.88	6.75	5.85	1.67	1.03	4.09	6.24
Not used	2.86	4.35	1.29	1.89	0.05	0.58	1.25	1.31	1.57	2.46
Unit total	149.03	448.48	80.42	152.24	34.53	26.22	45.89	126.01	68.61	296.24

Central Hardwood

Table 14.—Continued

(In thousand tons, green weight)

Forest Inventory Unit and disposition	Residue type									
	Total all residues		Total wood residue		Wood residue				Bark	
					Coarse[a]		Fine[b]			
	Softwood	Hardwood	Softwood	Hardwood	Softwood	Hardwood	Softwood	Hardwood	Softwood	Hardwood
Fiber products	0.07	2.56	0.07	2.56	0.07	2.56	–	–	–	–
Industrial fuel	23.97	44.33	9.83	17.44	0.99	3.60	8.85	13.84	14.14	26.89
Residential fuel	4.73	27.60	4.07	23.51	3.75	21.59	0.33	1.92	0.66	4.09
Mulch	0.12	1.57	0.06	0.54	–	–	0.06	0.54	0.06	1.03
Animal bedding	1.72	14.15	1.72	12.83	0.03	5.47	1.69	7.36	0.00	1.32
Miscellaneous[c]	5.84	23.71	4.17	15.06	2.33	5.84	1.83	9.23	1.67	8.65
Not used	0.13	0.87	0.10	0.76	0.05	0.30	0.05	0.46	0.03	0.11
Unit total	36.58	114.81	20.02	72.70	7.22	39.36	12.80	33.34	16.56	42.11
Northern Pine										
Fiber products	140.03	12.33	140.03	12.33	140.03	12.33	–	–	–	–
Industrial fuel	120.01	259.02	45.57	65.19	17.73	12.90	27.84	52.29	74.44	193.83
Residential fuel	12.76	34.63	10.05	28.60	8.05	24.60	2.00	4.00	2.71	6.03
Mulch	15.52	4.52	1.04	2.05	0.29	2.01	0.75	0.05	14.48	2.47
Animal bedding	77.98	13.50	77.63	11.63	0.24	0.88	77.39	10.75	0.35	1.87
Miscellaneous[c]	10.56	14.72	8.85	11.95	4.81	6.76	4.05	5.19	1.71	2.77
Not used	0.93	6.96	0.73	6.65	0.36	0.81	0.37	5.84	0.20	0.31
Unit total	377.79	345.68	283.91	138.40	171.51	60.29	112.40	78.11	93.88	207.28
Prairie										
Fiber products	–	0.00	–	0.00	–	0.00	–	0.00	–	0.00
Industrial fuel	0.01	4.53	0.01	4.35	0.01	4.30	0.00	0.04	0.00	0.18

Table 14.—Continued

(In thousand tons, green weight)

Forest Inventory Unit and disposition	Total all residues		Total wood residue		Residue type					
					Wood residue					
					Coarse[a]		Fine[b]		Bark	
	Softwood	Hardwood	Softwood	Hardwood	Softwood	Hardwood	Softwood	Hardwood	Softwood	Hardwood
Residential fuel	0.05	4.00	0.04	3.23	0.04	3.23	—	—	0.01	0.77
Mulch	—	0.00	—	0.00	—	—	—	0.00	—	0.00
Animal bedding	0.01	0.56	0.01	0.19	—	0.00	0.01	0.19	0.00	0.37
Miscellaneous[c]	0.03	6.10	0.02	4.19	0.01	0.37	0.01	3.82	0.01	1.91
Not used	0.01	0.47	0.01	0.28	0.00	0.14	0.01	0.14	0.00	0.19
Unit total	0.11	15.66	0.09	12.24	0.06	8.04	0.03	4.20	0.02	3.42

[a] Suitable for chipping such as slabs, edgings, veneer cores, etc.

[b] Not suitable for chipping such as sawdust, veneer clippings etc.

[c] Small dimension, specialty items, etc.

All table cells without observations are indicated by — . Table value of 0.00 indicates the volume rounds to less than 50 green tons. Columns and rows may not add to their totals due to rounding.